THE BEST
OF BERTRAND RUSSELL

For more than fifty years, in more than one hundred books and articles, Bertrand Russell has attacked dogmatic authority as an obstacle to human advancement, with wit, brilliance and lucidity. He has gained international eminence as a scientist, philosopher and social critic, and his sometimes unpopular opinions have aroused storms of controversy.

This stimulating and provocative book offers some of his best writings on a wide variety of subjects—psychology, politics, education, religion, ethics and marriage.

Unconventional, outspoken and original, these pieces display Bertrand Russell's genius for exposing the suspicion, fear, lust for power, hatred and intolerance which stand in the way of a better society.

A philosopher who is scientific, yet humane, hopeful and honest, Lord Russell has received many honors for his work, including the Order of Merit and the Nobel Prize for Literature.

THIS IS A REPRINT OF THE ORIGINAL HARDCOVER EDITION PUBLISHED BY GEORGE ALLEN AND UNWIN LTD.

The following books by Bertrand Russell are in print in the United States. Those marked with an asterisk are published in England by George Allen & Unwin Ltd.

ABC of Relativity (Oxford University Press; New American Library)
Analysis of Matter* (Dover)
Analysis of Mind* (Humanities Press)
Authority and the Individual* (Beacon Press)
Basic Writings (Simon & Schuster)
Bertrand Russell's Dictionary of Mind, Matter and Morals (Citadel)
Common Sense and Nuclear Warfare (Simon & Schuster)
The Conquest of Happiness* (Liveright; New American Library)
Critical Exposition of the Philosophy of Leibniz* (Humanities Press)
Education and the Good Life (Liveright)
Education and the Social Order* (Humanities Press)
Essay on the Foundation of Geometry (Dover)
Fact and Fiction (Simon & Schuster)
Freedom versus Organization* (Norton)
German Social Democracy (Simon & Schuster)
Has Man a Future? (Simon & Schuster)
History of Western Philosophy* (Simon & Schuster)
Human Knowledge* (Simon & Schuster)
Human Society in Ethics and Politics* (New American Library)
In Praise of Idleness* (Barnes & Noble)
An Inquiry into Meaning and Truth* (Humanities Press; Penguin)
Introduction to Mathematical Philosophy* (Humanities Press)
Knights of Bushido (Dutton)
Logic and Knowledge* (Macmillan)
Marriage and Morals* (Liveright; Bantam)
My Philosophical Development (Simon & Schuster)
Mysticism and Logic* (Barnes & Noble; Doubleday)
New Hopes for a Changing World (Humanities Press)
On the Philosophy of Science (Bobbs-Merrill)
Our Knowledge of the External World* (Humanities Press; New American Library)
Outline of Philosophy* (Meridian Books)
Philosophical Essays (Simon & Schuster)
Political Ideals (Simon & Schuster; Barnes & Noble)
Portraits from Memory* (Simon & Schuster)
Power: A New Social Analysis* (Barnes & Noble)
The Practice and Theory of Bolshevism* (Simon & Schuster)
The Principles of Mathematics* (Norton)
Principles of Social Reconstruction* (Humanities Press)
Problem of China (Humanities Press)
Problems of Philosophy (Oxford University Press)
Prospects of Industrial Civilization (Humanities Press)
Religion and Science (Oxford University Press)
Roads to Freedom* (Barnes & Noble)
Sceptical Essays* (Barnes & Noble)
The Scientific Outlook (Norton)
Selected Papers (Modern Library)
Unarmed Victory* (Simon & Schuster; Penguin)
Understanding History (Philosophical Library)
Unpopular Essays* (Simon & Schuster)
Why I Am Not a Christian* (Simon & Schuster)
Wisdom of the West (Doubleday; Fawcett)

Bertrand Russell's Best

SILHOUETTES IN SATIRE

Selected and Introduced by
PROFESSOR ROBERT E. EGNER

A MENTOR BOOK
Published by THE NEW AMERICAN LIBRARY

*Published as a MENTOR BOOK
by arrangement with George Allen & Unwin Ltd.,
who have authorized this softcover edition.*

SIXTH PRINTING

A handsome clothbound edition of this
work is obtainable from George Allen &
Unwin Ltd., *London,* 40 Museum Street,
W. C. 1; *Auckland,* 24 Wyndham Street;
Bombay, 15 Graham Road, Ballard Estate,
Bombay 1; *Calcutta,* 17 Chittaranjan Avenue,
Calcutta 13; *Cape Town,* 109 Long Street;
Karachi, 254 Ingle Road; *New Delhi,* 13-14
Ajmeri Gate Extension, New Delhi 1;
São Paulo, Avenida 9 de Julho, 1138-Ap. 51;
Sydney, N. S. W., Bradbury House, 55 York
Street; *Toronto,* 91 Wellington Street West.

Library of Congress Catalog Card No. 58-12839

MENTOR TRADEMARK REG. U.S. PAT. OFF. AND FOREIGN COUNTRIES
REGISTERED TRADEMARK——MARCA REGISTRADA
HECHO EN CHICAGO, U.S.A.

*MENTOR BOOKS are published by
The New American Library, Inc.
1301 Avenue of the Americas, New York, New York 10019*

PRINTED IN THE UNITED STATES OF AMERICA

PREFACE

Bertrand Russell needs no special introduction to the general reader; his pen has been active for over half a century and his more than one hundred books and articles have travelled a range of thought as wide as the scope of man's quest of knowledge. Lord Russell's position on the great variety of social problems he has written about has always been scientific in the sense that he does not claim pontifical certainty on the views expressed.

Is there a central key to an understanding of the social philosophy of Lord Russell? Is there a certain point that the general reader, who is not accustomed to philosophical jargon, should begin if he is to read with comprehension and insight? In terms of lucidity, style, and content, the many books and articles from which the material for the present volume was taken amply testify that Lord Russell has no peer among contemporary writers. What makes the selections in this book unique, however, is the incisive wit that Lord Russell brings to bear upon such varied subjects as religion, education, ethics, politics, psychology, and marriage. It is seldom that a philosopher can simultaneously display intellectual brilliance and humour.

Although Lord Russell has been the victim of extreme bigotry during the past fifty years, the attacks have not in any way caused him to recant his liberal views. In our own time few thinkers have been more flagrantly misrepresented than Lord Russell. Countless people have been influenced to envisage him as the anti-Christ, the idol smasher, and the patron philosopher of immorality. It is a portrait drawn in fear and prejudice. The fact that he has consistently pleaded for more benevolence in ethics and politics has escaped the notice of many of his critics. He maintains that what men need is not dogma, but rather an attitude of 'Christian love or compassion.' Lord Russell's critics pass over his statements to this effect in silence.

As these pages will show, Lord Russell has been mainly concerned with showing how dogmatic authority in its innumerable forms has been, and still remains, one of the great obstacles to human advancement, in terms of an increase in scientific knowledge on the one hand and a decrease in human misery on the other. These selections are witty, but the message beneath the humour is deadly serious. If the reader finds nothing more than wit, he is careless and superficial, seeing only the farcical elements before his eyes, and neglecting relations and perspective. One may hold a penny so that it hides the sun.

One might say that there are three Bertrand Russells. There are (1) the experimental investigator, (2) the social critic, and (3) the Voltairean satirist. Sometimes Lord Russell keeps these three selves in unison. But, more often than not, he allows the satirist full expression.

It was in his role as experimental investigator that he made his monumental contribution to mathematical philosophy which gained for him an international reputation as one of the great mathematicians of the twentieth century. The social and political problems of World War I, however, turned his attention from philosophy and science to social phenomena, and much of his later writing deals exclusively with social and political problems. He uses a swift and sharp wit to express and expose the evil passions in human minds —suspicion, fear, lust for power, hatred, and intolerance—which stand in the way of a more benevolent society. He is an inspired thinker who has just the right measure of wit to spice his wisdom. Russell, however, possesses one cardinal virtue which is rare among social critics; his criticism is always constructive despite, what appears to some, a destructive tone. He does not wantonly destroy an edifice, nor does he dismantle an institution without showing how to build a better one. Above all the reader will find Lord Russell scientific, yet humane, hopeful, and thoroughly honest. Lord Russell is, in short, the greatest combiner of *Common sense* and *uncommon sense*, the undisputed heir of a tradition in British philosophy that extends from Francis Bacon. Among the many honours that Lord Russell has received are the much esteemed Order of Merit, bestowed upon him by King George VI in 1949, and the equally esteemed Nobel Prize for Literature in 1950.

This book is an anthology of witticisms on a variety of topics—psychology, politics, education, religion, ethics and marriage. The selections are taken from a large number of Lord Russell's books and articles. The choice of selections is the editor's, and he is responsible for the abridgement of exposition and argument. No attempt was made to include every witticism available; in his opinion, this is *Bertrand Russell's Best*.

Contents

MEANING OF SYMBOLS

Books

I

PSYCHOLOGY

A NUMBER OF THE SELECTIONS in this chapter are taken from Lord Russell's Nobel Prize Acceptance Speech, delivered at Stockholm in 1950. In this lecture his keen observation and sharp wit are focused on human passions and their effect upon mankind. Such topics as vanity, power, and the love of excitement are stripped of their customary trappings and laid out in the nude to lie in state.

Few modern thinkers dare be as candid in the expression of unwelcomed thoughts as Lord Russell. His attitude is uncompromising: he is not afraid to run the risk of discussing 'sacred' matters in spite of the fact that his free views have exposed him to repeated attacks by bigots and obscurantists. Those who fear the embarrassment of having their noble façade dismantled quite naturally rebel against anyone who suggests a critical examination of their motives and beliefs.

Human nature has changed little since the time of primitive man. Our understanding of the forces which control behaviour, however, has increased immeasurably with the development of scientific methods of inquiry in the field of psychology. Only a century ago psychology was completely unscientific; now psychology is an independent science, the latest discipline to be separated from philosophy. Lord Russell maintains, however, that our knowledge of psychology has not been used to its fullest advantage in solving the ancient problem of how men can live together in peace.

In his *Nobel Prize Lecture* Lord Russell says the
fundamental motives that appeal to most men are 'acquisitiveness,' 'vanity,' 'rivalry,' and 'love of power.'
In politics, for example, the springs of human action
are derived from these basic drives. The political leader
who can convince the populace that he can satisfy
these desires can sway masses of men to believe that
two and two are five and that his authority is divinely
sanctioned. The political leader who ignores these
basic motives is usually destitute of popular support.
The psychology of mob dynamics is an essential part
in the education of successful political leaders.

The study of scientific psychology affords an indispensable tool for helping men solve some of their
gravest problems in creating a better world. If Lord
Russell's wit brings them out in the open, it will have
served its purpose.

Vanity is a motive of immense potency. Anyone who has much to do with children knows how they are constantly performing some antic, and saying, 'Look at me.' 'Look at me' is one of the fundamental desires of the human heart. It can take innumerable forms, from buffoonery to the pursuit of posthumous fame. There was a Renaissance Italian princeling who was asked by the priest on his death-bed if he had anything to repent of. 'Yes,' he said, 'there is one thing. On one occasion I had a visit from the Emperor and the Pope simultaneously. I took them to the top of my tower to see the view, and I neglected the opportunity to throw them both down, which would have given me immortal fame.' History does not relate whether the priest gave him absolution. (N. P. A. S.)

I once befriended two little girls from Esthonia, who had narrowly escaped death from starvation in a famine. They lived in my family, and of course had plenty to eat. But they spent all their leisure visiting neighbouring farms and stealing potatoes, which they hoarded. Rockefeller, who in his infancy had experienced great poverty, spent his adult life in a similar manner. (N. P. A. S.)

Human beings show their superiority to the brutes by their capacity for boredom, though I have sometimes thought in examining the apes at the zoo, that they, perhaps, have the rudiments of this tiresome emotion. However that may be, experience shows that escape from boredom is one of the really powerful desires of almost all human beings. When white men first effect contact with some unspoilt race of savages, they offer them all kinds of benefits, from the light of the gospel to pumpkin pie. These, however, much as we may regret it, most savages receive with indifference. What they really value among the gifts that we bring to them is intoxicating liquor, which enables them for the first time in their lives to have the illusion, for a few brief moments, that it is better to be alive than dead. (N. P. A. S.)

What vanity needs for its satisfaction is glory, and it is easy to have glory without power. The people who enjoy the greatest glory in the United States are film stars, but they can be put in their place by the committee for Un-American Activities, which enjoys no glory whatever. (N. P. A. S.)

The desire for excitement is very deep-seated in human beings, especially in males. I suppose that in the hunting stage it was more easily gratified than it has been since. The chase was exciting, war was exciting, courtship was exciting. A savage will manage to commit adultery with a woman while her husband is asleep beside her. This situation, I imagine, is not boring. But with the coming of agriculture life began to grow dull, except, of course, for the aristocrats, who remained, and still remain, in the hunting stage. (C. H., page 57.)

The completely untravelled person will view all foreigners as the savage regards a member of another herd. But the man who has travelled, or who has studied international politics, will have discovered that, if the herd is to prosper, it must, to some degree, become amalgamated with other herds. If you are English and someone says to you: 'The French are your brothers,' your first instinctive feeling will be: 'Nonsense, they shrug their shoulders, and talk French.

And I am even told that they eat frogs.' If he explains to you that one may have to fight the Russians, that, if so, it will be desirable to defend the line of the Rhine, and that, if the line of the Rhine is to be defended, the help of the French is essential, you will begin to see what he means when he says that the French are your brothers. But if some fellow-traveller were to go on to say that the Russians also are your brothers, he would be unable to persuade you, unless he could show that we are in danger from the Martians. We love those who hate our enemies, and if we had no enemies there would be very few people whom we should love. (N. P. A. S.)

Civilized life has grown altogether too tame, and, if it is to be stable, it must provide harmless outlets for the impulses which our remote ancestors satisfied in hunting. In Australia, where people are few and rabbits are many, I watched a whole populace satisfying the primitive impulse in the primitive manner by the skilful slaughter of many thousands of rabbits. But in London or New York, where people are many and rabbits are few, some other means must be found to gratify primitive impulse. I think every big town should contain artificial waterfalls that people could descend in very fragile canoes, and they should contain bathing pools full of mechanical sharks. Any person found advocating a preventive war should be condemned to two hours a day with these ingenious monsters. (N. P. A. S.)

Every isolated passion is, in isolation, insane; sanity may be defined as a synthesis of insanities. Every dominant passion generates a dominant fear, the fear of its non-fulfilment. Every dominant fear generates a nightmare, sometimes in the form of an explicit and conscious fanaticism, sometimes in a paralysing timidity, sometimes in an unconscious or subconscious terror which finds expression only in dreams. The man who wishes to preserve sanity in a dangerous world should summon in his own mind a parliament of fears, in which each in turn is voted absurd by all the others. (N. E. P., introduction.)

The frequency with which a man experiences lust depends upon his own physical condition, whereas the occasions which rouse such feelings in him depend upon the social conventions to which he is accustomed. To an early Victorian man a woman's ankles were sufficient stimulus, whereas a modern man remains unmoved by anything up to the thigh. This is merely a question of fashion in clothing. If nakedness were the fashion, it would cease to excite us, and women would be forced, as they are in certain savage tribes, to adopt clothing as a means of making themselves sexually attractive. Exactly similar considerations apply to literature and pictures: what was exciting in the Victorian Age would leave the men of a franker epoch quite unmoved. The more prudes restrict the permissible degree of sexual appeal, the less is required to make such an appeal effective. Nine-tenths of the appeal of pornography is due to the indecent feelings concerning sex which moralists inculcate in the young; the other tenth is physiological, and will occur in one way or another whatever the state of the law may be. On these grounds, although I fear that few will agree with me, I am firmly persuaded that there ought to be no law whatsoever on the subject of obscene publications. (M. M., pages 115–116.)

Men who allow their love of power to give them a distorted view of the world are to be found in every asylum: one man will think he is the Governor of the Bank of England, another will think he is the

King, and yet another will think he is God. Highly similar delusions, if expressed by educated men in obscure language, lead to professorships of philosophy; and if expressed by emotional men in eloquent language, lead to dictatorships. (P.: A. N. S. A., page 259.)

Anthropologists have described how Papuan head hunters, deprived by white authority of their habitual sport, lose all zest, and are no longer able to be interested in anything. I do not wish to infer that they should have been allowed to go on hunting heads, but I do mean that it would have been worth while if psychologists had taken some trouble to find some innocent substitute activity. Civilized Man everywhere is, to some degree, in the position of the Papuan victims of virtue. We have all kinds of aggressive impulses, and also creative impulses, which society forbids us to indulge, and the alternatives that it supplies in the shape of football matches and all-in wrestling are hardly adequate. Anyone who hopes that in time it may be possible to abolish war should give serious thought to the problem of satisfying harmlessly the instincts that we inherit from long generations of savages. For my part I find a sufficient outlet in detective stories, where I alternately identify myself with the murderer and the huntsman-detective, but I know there are those to whom this vicarious outlet is too mild, and for them something stronger should be provided. (A. I., page 8.)

In Lisbon when heretics were publicly burned, it sometimes happened that one of them, by particularly edifying recantation, would be granted the boon of being strangled before being put into the flames. This would make the spectators so furious that the authorities had great difficulty in preventing them from lynching the penitent and burning him on their own account. The spectacle of the writhing torments of the victims was, in fact, one of the principal pleasures to which the populace looked forward to enliven a somewhat drab existence. I cannot doubt that this pleasure greatly contributed to the general belief that the burning of heretics was a righteous act. The same sort of thing applies to war. People who are vigorous and brutal often find war enjoyable, provided that it is a victorious war and that there is not too much interference with rape and plunder. This is a great help in persuading people that wars are righteous. (U. E., page 147.)

In order to be happy we require all kinds of supports to our self-esteem. We are human beings, therefore human beings are the purpose of creation. We are Americans, therefore America is God's own country. We are white, and therefore God cursed Ham and his descendants who were black. We are Protestant or Catholic, as the case may be, therefore Catholics or Protestants, as the case may be, are an abomination. We are male, and therefore women are unreasonable; or female, and therefore men are brutes. We are Easterners, and therefore the West is wild and woolly; or Westerners, and therefore the East is effete. We work with our brains, and therefore it is the educated classes that are important; or we work with our hands, and therefore manual labour alone gives dignity. Finally, and above all, we each have one merit which is entirely unique: we are Ourself. With these comforting reflections we go out to do battle with the world; without them our courage might fail. Without them, as things are, we should feel inferior because we have not learned the sentiment of equality. If we could feel genuinely that we are the equals of our neighbours, neither their betters nor their inferiors, perhaps life would become less of a battle, and we should need less in the way of intoxicating myth to give us Dutch courage. (U. E., page 160.)

There was, until the end of the eighteenth century, a theory that insanity is due to possession by devils. It was inferred that any pain suffered by the patient is also suffered by the devils, so that the best cure is to make the patient suffer so much that the devils will decide to abandon him. The insane, in accordance with this theory, were savagely beaten. This treatment was tried on King George III when he was mad, but without success. It is a curious and painful fact that almost all the completely futile treatments that have been believed in during the long history of medical folly have been such as caused acute suffering to the patient. When anaesthetics were discovered pious people considered them an attempt to evade the will of God. It was pointed out, however, that when God extracted Adam's rib He put him into a deep sleep. This proved that anaesthetics are all right for *men*; women, however, ought to suffer because of the curse of Eve. In the West votes for women proved this doctrine mistaken, but in Japan, to this day, women in childbirth are not allowed any alleviation through anaesthetics. As the Japanese do not believe in Genesis, this piece of sadism must have some other justification. (U. E., page 87.)

By self-interest Man has become gregarious, but in instinct he has remained to a great extent solitary; hence the need of religion and morality to reinforce self-interest. But the habit of foregoing present satisfactions for the sake of future advantages is irksome, and when passions are roused the prudent restraints of social behaviour become difficult to endure. Those who, at such times, throw them off, acquire a new

energy and sense of power from the cessation of inner
conflict, and, though they may come to disaster in
the end, enjoy meanwhile a sense of god-like exalta-
tion which, though known to the great mystics, can
never be experienced by a merely pedestrian virtue.
The solitary part of their nature reasserts itself, but
if the intellect survives the reassertion must clothe
itself in myth. The mystic becomes one with God, and
in the contemplation of the infinite feels himself ab-
solved from duty to his neighbour. The anarchic rebel
does even better: he feels himself not one with God,
but God. Truth and duty, which represent our sub-
jection to matter and to our neighbours, exist no
longer for the man who has become God; for others,
truth is what *he* posits, duty what *he* commands. If
we could all live solitary and without labour, we could
all enjoy this ecstasy of independence; since we cannot, its delights are only available to madmen and
dictators. (H. W. P., pages 681–682.)

Happiness is promoted by associations of persons with
similar tastes and similar opinions. Social intercourse
may be expected to develop more and more along
these lines, and it may be hoped that by these means
the loneliness that now afflicts so many unconventional
people will be gradually diminished almost to vanish-
ing point. This will undoubtedly increase their happiness, but it will of course diminish the sadistic pleasure
which the conventional at present derive from having
the unconventional at their mercy. I do not think,
however, that this is a pleasure which we need be
greatly concerned to preserve. (C. H., page 138.)

Our mental make-up is suited to a life of very severe
physical labour. I used, when I was younger, to take
my holidays walking. I would cover 25 miles a day,
and when the evening came I had no need of anything

to keep me from boredom, since the delight of sitting amply sufficed. But modern life cannot be conducted on these physically strenuous principles. A great deal of work is sedentary, and most manual work exercises only a few specialized muscles. When crowds assemble in Trafalgar Square to cheer to the echo an announcement that the government has decided to have them killed, they would not do so if they had all walked 25 miles that day. This cure for bellicosity is, however, impracticable, and if the human race is to survive—a thing which is, perhaps, undesirable—other means must be found for securing an innocent outlet for the unused physical energy that produces love of excitement. This is a matter which has been too little considered, both by moralists and by social reformers. The social reformers are of the opinion that they have more serious things to consider. The moralists, on the other hand, are immensely impressed with the seriousness of all the permitted outlets of the love of excitement; the seriousness, however, in their minds, is that of Sin. Dance halls, cinemas, this age of jazz, are all, if we may believe our ears, gateways to Hell, and we should be better employed sitting at home contemplating our sins. I find myself unable to be in entire agreement with the grave men who utter these warnings. The devil has many forms, some designed to deceive the young, some designed to deceive the old and serious. If it is the devil that tempts the young to enjoy themselves, is it not, perhaps, the same personage that persuades the old to condemn their enjoyment? And is not condemnation perhaps merely a form of excitement appropriate to old age? And is it not, perhaps, a drug which—like opium—has to be taken in continually stronger doses to produce the desired effect? Is it not to be feared that, beginning with the wickedness of the cinema, we should be led step by step to condemn the opposite political party, dagoes, wops, Asiatics, and, in short, everybody except the fellow members of our club? And it is from just such condemnations, when widespread, that wars proceed. I have never heard of a war that proceeded from dance halls. (N. P. A. S.)

There is no greater reason for children to honour parents than for parents to honour children, except that while the children are young, the parents are stronger than the children. The same thing, of course, happened in the relations of men and women. It was the duty of wives to submit to husbands, not of husbands to submit to wives. The only basis for this view was that if wives could be induced to accept it, it saved trouble for their husbands. 'The man is not of the woman, but the woman of the man; neither was the man created for the woman, but the woman for the man' (I Cor. xi. 8, 9). I defy anyone to find any basis for this view, except that men have stronger muscles than women. (N. H. C. W., pages 68–69.)

A large proportion of the human race, it is true, is obliged to work so hard in obtaining necessaries that little energy is left over for other purposes; but those whose livelihood is assured do not, on that account, cease to be active. Xerxes had no lack of food or raiment or wives at the time when he embarked upon the Athenian expedition. Newton was certain of material comfort from the moment when he became a Fellow of Trinity, but it was after this that he wrote the *Principia*. St. Francis and Ignatius Loyola had no need to found Orders to escape from want. These were eminent men, but the same characteristic, in varying degrees, is to be found in all but a small exceptionally sluggish minority. Mrs. A, who is quite sure of her husband's success in business, and has no fear of the workhouse, likes to be better dressed than Mrs. B, although she could escape the danger of pneumonia at much less expense. (P.: A. N. S. A., pages 9–10.)

Some astronomers try to cheer us up in moments of depression by assuring us that one fine day the sun will explode, and in the twinkling of an eye we shall all be turned into gas. I do not know whether this is going to happen, nor when it will happen if it does happen, but I think it is safe to say that if it does it will be a matter outside human control, and that even the best astronomers will be unable to prevent it. This is an extreme example, and one which it is useless to think about, because there is no way in which human behaviour can be adapted to it. It does, however, serve one purpose, which is to remind us that we are not gods. You may exclaim indignantly, 'but I never thought we were!' No doubt, dear reader, you are not one of those who suffer from the most extreme follies of our age, for if you were, you would not be one of my readers. But if you consider the Politbureau or the American technocrats you will see that there are those who escape atheism by impiously imagining themselves on the throne of the Almighty. (N. H. C. W., pages 26–27.)

Mass hysteria is a phenomenon not confined to human beings; it may be seen in any gregarious species. I once saw a photograph of a large herd of wild elephants in Central Africa seeing an aeroplane for the first time, and all in a state of wild collective terror. The elephant, at most times, is a calm and sagacious beast, but this unprecedented phenomenon of a noisy, unknown animal in the sky had thrown the whole herd completely off its balance. Each separate animal was terrified, and its terror communicated itself to the others, causing a vast multiplication of panic. As, however, there were no journalists among them, the terror died down when the aeroplane was out of sight. (T. F. D., page 7.)

The criminal law has, from the point of view of thwarted virtue, the merit of allowing an outlet for those impulses of aggression which cowardice, disguised as morality, restrains in their more spontaneous forms. War has the same merit. You must not kill your neighbour, whom perhaps you genuinely hate, but by a little propaganda this hate can be transferred to some foreign nation, against whom all your murderous impulses become patriotic heroism. (N. H. C. W., page 175.)

If you ask a modern anti-Semite why he dislikes Jews, he will tell you that they are unscrupulous and sharp in business and merciless to their debtors; he will tell you that they are always on the make, always intriguing, always supporting each other against Gentile competitors. If you say you have sometimes found similar characteristics among Christians, the anti-Semite will say: 'Oh, of course I don't deny there are ruffians who are not Jews. And I have some very good friends among Jews. But I am speaking of the average.' If you question him when he is off his guard, you will find that whenever a Jew engages in a bit of sharp practice he says, 'how like a Jew,' but when a Gentile does likewise he says 'and, you know, the astonishing thing is that he is not a Jew.' This is not a scientific method of arriving at averages. (N. H. C. W., pages 102–103.)

Young men and young women meet each other with much less difficulty than was formerly the case, and every housemaid expects at least once a week as much excitement as would have lasted a Jane Austen heroine throughout a whole novel. (c. h., page 59.)

Everybody has had at some time nightmares of falling, which seem to suggest an origin in the lives of our arboreal ancestors, though this perhaps is fanciful. Hymns and myths tend to speak of refuges from storm and of images of water in a parched land. Moses striking the rock makes a universal appeal, even to those who have never been very thirsty. Hymns represent heaven as a refuge from the storms of life, not as a place where one escapes the dangers of being run over by a motor-bus, although the latter danger is a much more frequent experience in modern urban life. (n. h. c. w., pages 163–164.)

Now, apart from arguments as to the proved fallibility of memory, there is one awkward consideration which the sceptic may urge. Remembering, which occurs now, cannot possibly—he may say—prove that what is remembered occurred at some other time, because the world might have sprung into being five minutes ago, exactly as it then was, full of acts of remembering which were entirely misleading. Opponents of Darwin, such as Edmund Gosse's father, urged a very similar argument against evolution. The world, they said, was created in 4004 b.c., complete with fossils, which were inserted to try our faith. The world was created suddenly, but was made such as it would have been if it had evolved. There is no logical impossibility about this view. And similarly there is no logical impossibility in the view that the world was created five minutes ago, complete with memories and records. This may seem an improbable hypothesis, but it is not logically refutable. (o. p., page 7.)

If I wish to travel by plane to New York, reason tells me that it is better to take a plane which is going to New York than one which is going to Constantinople. I suppose that those who think me unduly rational, consider that I ought to become so agitated at the airport as to jump into the first plane that I see, and when it lands me in Constantinople I ought to curse the people among whom I find myself for being Turks and not Americans. This would be a fine, full-blooded way of behaving, and would, I suppose, meet with the commendation of my critics. (H. S. E. P., preface, pages 8–9.)

My first advice (on how *not* to grow old) would be to choose your ancestors carefully. Although both my parents died young, I have done well in this respect as regards my other ancestors. My maternal grandfather, it is true, was cut off in the flower of his youth at the age of sixty-seven, but my other three grandparents all lived to be over eighty. Of remoter ancestors I can only discover one who did not live to a great age, and he died of a disease which is now rare, namely, having his head cut off. (P. F. M., p. 50.)

. . . The difference between mind and brain is not a difference of quality, but a difference of arrangement. It is like the difference between arranging people in geographical order or in alphabetical order, both of which are done in the post office directory. The same people are arranged in both cases, but in quite different contexts. In like manner the context of a visual sensation for physics is physical, and outside the brain. Going backward, it takes you to the eye, and thence to a photon and thence to a quantum transition in some distant object. The context of the visual sensation for psychology is quite

different. Suppose, for example, the visual sensation
is that of a telegram saying that you are ruined. A
number of events will take place in your mind in accordance with the laws of psychological causation,
and it may be quite a long time before there is any
purely physical effect, such as tearing your hair, or
exclaiming 'Woe is me!' (P. F. M., pages 159–160.)

II

RELIGION

WITH THE PUBLICATION IN 1903 of Lord Russell's often quoted essay, 'A Free Man's Worship,' his views on religion have been closely followed by most writers on this subject. His position on religion has changed little since this time, but the evidence for belief in traditional religious dogma has not undergone any great change either.

Whether or not one agrees with Lord Russell's views on religious orthodoxy, one thing is clear: his opinions are so lucidly stated that, even when one disagrees with him, one knows precisely what it is with which one is disagreeing. Lord Russell does not, as some philosophers do, create an atmosphere of mysticism about the meaning of what he says. Lord Russell has never been opposed to those for whom mythology is a cultural characteristic; he has been opposed, however, to those who adopt persecution as a means of propagating their beliefs.

The history of organized religion in the West affords a number of instances in which religion has opposed humanitarian and scientific progress. A number of advances in medicine, for example, would have been achieved sooner if free inquiry had been common, and orthodox thinking habits had been rare. Only a century ago there were many who believed that certain diseases were caused by sin, and that it was good that the wicked should suffer for their sins. Anyone who dared suggest some other cause of these diseases was subject to various forms of censorship.

People in Western countries are not burned at the stake for disagreeing with prevailing religious dogma as they were in former times, but they are still subject to other, more refined, forms of unkindness. The psychological impact on religious minorities (especially the younger members of these groups) of being merely 'tolerated' by the majority group is a case in point. Agnostics, for instance, are not entirely free to admit their beliefs publicly without suffering some kind of unpleasant consequences. In some cases this may mean discrimination in obtaining employment by one who is otherwise fully qualified, while in other cases it may mean loss of standing in a community if it were known that one confessed not believing in God. Those who claim that religious freedom is a necessary condition for a democratic society sometimes forget that tolerance means more than a concordat between the adherents of rival creeds. Religious liberty implies equal tolerance towards those who profess no dogma whatever.

Religion, if it is not to be harmful, must be free of dangerous elements—suspicion, fear, and hate—which lead step by step to organized persecution. The selections which follow illustrate again that serious thought and keen humour make an excellent partnership; seldom in the history of letters does one find such amazing fusion of insight and wit.

I observe that a very large portion of the human race does not believe in God and suffers no visible punishment in consequence. And if there were a God, I think it very unlikely that he would have such an uneasy vanity as to be offended by those who doubt his existence. (w. a.)

Although we are taught the Copernican astronomy in our textbooks, it has not yet penetrated to our religion or our morals, and has not even succeeded in destroying belief in astrology. People still think that the Divine Plan has special reference to human beings, and that a special Providence not only looks after the good, but also punishes the wicked. I am sometimes shocked by the blasphemies of those who think themselves pious—for instance, the nuns who never take a bath without wearing a bathrobe all the time. When asked why, since no man can see them, they reply: 'Oh, but you forget the good God.' Apparently they conceive of the Deity as a Peeping Tom, whose omnipotence enables Him to see through bathroom walls, but who is foiled by bathrobes. This view strikes me as curious. (u. e., pages 75–76.)

Christians hold that their faith does good, but other faiths do harm. At any rate, they hold this about the Communist faith. What I wish to maintain is that *all* faiths do harm. We may define 'faith' as a firm belief in something for which there is no evidence. When there is evidence, no one speaks of 'faith.' We do not speak of faith that two and two are four or that the earth is round. We only speak of faith when we wish to substitute emotion for evidence. (h. s. e. p., page 215.)

The Church attacked the habit of the bath on the ground that everything which makes the body more attractive tends towards sin. Dirt was praised, and the odour of sanctity became more and more penetrating. 'The purity of the body and its garments,' said St. Paula, 'means the impurity of the soul.' (Havelock Ellis, *Studies in the Psychology of Sex*, Vol. IV, p. 31.) Lice were called the pearls of God, and to be covered with them was an indispensable mark of a holy man. (M. M., pages 48–49.)

Since evolution became fashionable, the glorification of Man has taken a new form. We are told that evolution has been guided by one great Purpose: through the millions of years when there were only slime, or trilobites, throughout the ages of dinosaurs and giant ferns, of bees and wild flowers, God was preparing the Great Climax. At last, in the fullness of time, He produced Man, including such specimens as Nero and Caligula, Hitler and Mussolini, whose transcendent glory justified the long painful process. For my part, I find even eternal damnation less incredible, certainly less ridiculous, than this lame and impotent conclusion which we are asked to admire as the supreme effort of Omnipotence. (U. E., page 84.)

Mankind . . . are a mistake. The universe would be sweeter and fresher without them. When the morning dew sparkles like diamonds in the rising sun of a September morning, there is beauty and exquisite purity in each blade of grass, and it is dreadful to think of this beauty being beheld by sinful eyes, which smirch its loveliness with their sordid and cruel ambitions. I cannot understand how God, who sees this loveliness, can have tolerated so long the baseness of those who boast blasphemously that they have been made in His image. Perhaps . . . it may yet fall to my lot to be the more thoroughgoing instrument of the Divine Purpose which was carried out half-heartedly in the days of Noah. (S. S., pages 48–49.)

It is not by prayer and humility that you cause things to go as you wish, but by acquiring a knowledge of natural laws. The power you acquire in this way is much greater and more reliable than that formerly supposed to be acquired by prayer, because you never could tell whether your prayer would be favourably heard in Heaven. The power of prayer, moreover, had recognized limits; it would have been impious to ask too much. But the power of science has no known limits. We were told that faith could remove mountains, but no one believed it; we are now told that the atomic bomb can remove mountains, and everyone believes it. (I. S. S., page 15.)

According to St. Thomas the soul is not transmitted with the semen, but is created afresh with each man. There is, it is true, a difficulty: when a man is born out of wedlock, this seems to make God an accomplice in adultery. This objection, however, is only specious. There is a grave objection which troubled St. Augustine, and that is as to the transmission of original sin. It is the soul that sins, and if the soul is not transmitted, but created afresh, how can it inherit the sin of Adam? This is not discussed by St. Thomas. (H. W. P., page 458.)

I am constantly asked: What can you, with your cold rationalism, offer to the seeker after salvation that is comparable to the cosy homelike comfort of a fenced-in dogmatic creed? To this the answer is many-sided. In the first place, I do not say that I can offer as much happiness as is to be obtained by the abdication of reason. I do not say that I can offer as much happiness as is to be obtained from drink or drugs or amassing great wealth by swindling widows and orphans. It is not the happiness of the individual convert that concerns me; it is the happiness of mankind. If you genuinely desire the happiness of mankind, certain forms of ignoble personal happiness are not open to you. If your child is ill, and you are a conscientious parent, you accept medical diagnosis, however doubtful and discouraging; if you accept the cheerful opinion of a quack and your child consequently dies, you are not excused by the pleasantness of belief in the quack while it lasted. (I. S. S., page 87.)

If everything must have a cause, then God must have a cause. If there can be anything without a cause, it may just as well be the world as God, so that there cannot be any validity in that argument. It is exactly of the same nature as the Indian's view, that the world rested upon an elephant and the elephant rested upon a tortoise; and when they said, 'How about the tortoise?' the Indian said, 'Suppose we change the subject.' The argument is really no better than that. (W. N. C., pages 6–7.)

The agnostic is not quite so certain as some Christians are as to what is good and what is evil. He does not hold, as most Christians in the past held, that people who disagree with the Government on abstruse points of theology ought to suffer a painful death. He is against persecution, and rather chary of moral condemnation.

As for 'sin,' he thinks it not a useful notion. He admits, of course, that some kinds of conduct are desirable and some undesirable, but he holds that the punishment of undesirable kinds is only to be commended when it is deterrent or reformatory, not when it is inflicted because it is thought a good thing on its own account that the wicked should suffer. It was this belief in vindictive punishment that made men accept hell. This is part of the harm done by the notion of 'sin.' (w. a.)

It was geology, Darwin, and the doctrine of evolution, that first upset the faith of British men of science. If man was evolved by insensible gradations from lower forms of life, a number of things became very difficult to understand. At what moment in evolution did our ancestors acquire free will? At what stage in the long journey from the amoeba did they begin to have immortal souls? When did they first become capable of the kinds of wickedness that would justify a benevolent Creator in sending them into eternal torment? Most people felt that such punishment would be hard on monkeys, in spite of their propensity for throwing coconuts at the heads of Europeans. But how about *Pithecanthropus Erectus?* Was it really he who ate the apple? Or was it *Homo Pekiniensis?* (u. e., pages 132–133.)

There is something feeble and a little contemptible about a man who cannot face the perils of life without the help of comfortable myths. Almost inevitably some part of him is aware that they are myths and that he believes them only because they are comforting. But he dare not face this thought! Moreover, since he is aware, however dimly, that his opinions are not rational, he becomes furious when they are disputed. (h. s. e. p., pages 219–20.)

What Galileo and Newton had done for astronomy Darwin did for biology. The adaptations of animals and plants to their environments were a favourite

theme of pious naturalists in the eighteenth and early
nineteenth centuries. These adaptations were explained
by the Divine Purpose. It is true that the explanation
was sometimes a little odd. If rabbits were theologians,
they might think the exquisite adaptation of weasels
to the killing of rabbits hardly a matter for thankful-
ness. And there was a conspiracy of silence about the
tapeworm. (I. S. S., pages 11–12.)

I do not understand where the 'beauty' and 'harmony'
of nature are supposed to be found. Throughout the
animal kingdom, animals ruthlessly prey upon each
other. Most of them are either cruelly killed by other
animals or slowly die of hunger. For my part, I am
unable to see any very great beauty or harmony in the
tapeworm. Let it not be said that this creature is sent
as a punishment for our sins, for it is more prevalent
among animals than among humans.

    I suppose what is meant by this 'beauty' and 'har-
mony' are such things as the beauty of the starry
heavens. But one should remember that the stars every
now and again explode and reduce everything in their
neighbourhood to a vague mist. (W. A.)

One of the last questions discussed by St. Thomas in
book four is the resurrection of the body. Here, as
elsewhere, Aquinas states very fairly the arguments
that have been brought against orthodox position. One
of these, at first sight, offers great difficulties. What
is to happen, asks the Saint, to a man who never,
throughout his life, ate anything but human flesh, and
whose parents did likewise? It would seem unfair to
his victims that they should be deprived of their bodies
at the last day as a consequence of his greed; yet, if
not, what will be left to make up his body? I am

happy to say that this difficulty, which might at first
sight seem insuperable, is triumphantly met. The iden-
tity of the body, St. Thomas points out, is not
dependent on the persistence of the same material
particles; during life, by the processes of eating and
digesting, the matter composing the body undergoes
perpetual change. The cannibal may, therefore, receive the same body at the resurrection, even if it is
not composed of the same matter as was in his body
when he died. With this comforting thought we may
end our abstract of the *Summa contra Gentiles*. (H.
W. P., page 461.)

There is little of the true philosophic spirit in Aquinas.
He does not, like the Platonic Socrates, set out to
follow wherever the argument may lead. He is not
engaged in an inquiry, the result of which it is impossible to know in advance. Before he begins to phi-
losophize, he already knows the truth; it is declared
in the Catholic faith. If he can find apparently rational
arguments for some parts of the faith, so much the
better; if he cannot, he need only fall back on revelation. The finding of arguments for a conclusion given
in advance is not philosophy, but special pleading. (H.
W. P., page 463.)

The raw fruits of the earth were made for human
sustenance. Even the white tails of rabbits, according
to some theologians, have a purpose, namely to make
it easier for sportsmen to shoot them. There are, it is
true, some inconveniences: lions and tigers are too
fierce, the summer is too hot, and the winter too cold.
But these things only began after Adam ate the apple;
before that, all animals were vegetarians, and the
season was always spring. If only Adam had been

content with peaches and nectarines, grapes and pears and pineapples, these blessings would still be ours. (U. E., page 83.)

According to St. Thomas, astrology is to be rejected, for the usual reasons. In answer to the question 'Is there such a thing as fate?' Aquinas replies that we *might* give the name 'fate' to the order impressed by Providence, but it is wiser not to do so, as 'fate' is a pagan word. This leads to an argument that prayer is useful although Providence is unchangeable (I have failed to follow this argument), God sometimes works miracles, but no one else can. Magic, however, is possible with the help of demons; this is not properly miraculous, and is not by the help of the stars. (H. W. P., page 459.)

How far has the American outlook on life and the world influenced Europe, and how far is it likely to do so?

And first of all: What is the distinctively American outlook? And what, in comparison, is the distinctively European outlook?

Traditionally, the European outlook may be said to be derived from astronomy. When Abraham watched his flocks by night, he observed the stars in their courses: they moved with a majestic regularity utterly remote from human control. When the Lord answered Job out of the whirlwind, He said: 'Canst thou bind the sweet influences of Pleiades, or loose the bands of Orion?' The reply was in the negative. Even more relevant is the question: 'Knowest thou the ordinances of heaven? Canst thou set the dominion thereof in the earth?' To which Job answered: 'Behold, I am vile; what shall I answer thee? I will lay my hand upon my mouth.' The conclusion is that man is a feeble creature, to whom only submission and worship are becoming. Pride is insolence, and belief in human power is impiety. (P. C. I., page 8.)

Nature, it is true, still sees to it that we are mortal, but with the progress in medicine it will become more and more common for people to live until they have had their fill of life. We are supposed to wish to live forever and to look forward to the unending joys of heaven, of which, by miracle, the monotony will never grow stale. But in fact, if you question any candid person who is no longer young, he is very likely to tell you that, having tasted life in this world, he has no wish to begin again as a 'new boy' in another. (U. E., page 147.)

We read in the Old Testament that it was a religious duty to exterminate conquered races completely, and that to spare even their cattle and sheep was an impiety. Dark terrors and misfortunes in the life to come oppressed the Egyptians and Etruscans, but never reached their full development until the victory of Christianity. Gloomy saints who abstained from all pleasures of sense, who lived in solitude in the desert, denying themselves meat and wine and the society of women, were, nevertheless, not obliged to abstain from *all* pleasures. The pleasures of the mind were considered to be superior to those of the body, and a high place among the pleasures of the mind was assigned to the contemplation of the eternal tortures to which the pagans and heretics would hereafter be subjected. (U. E., page 149.)

The standpoint of modern liberal theologians is well set forth by Dr. Tennant in his book *The Concept of*

Sin. According to him sin consists in acts of will that are in conscious opposition to a known law, the moral law being known by Revelation as God's will. It follows that a man destitute of religion cannot sin. (H. S. E. P., page 94.)

One occasion for theological intervention to prevent the mitigation of human suffering was the discovery of anaesthetics. Simpson, in 1847, recommended their use in childbirth, and was immediately reminded by the clergy that God said to Eve: 'In sorrow shalt thou bring forth children' (Gen. iii. 16). And how could she sorrow if she was under the influence of chloroform? Simpson succeeded in proving that there was no harm in giving anaesthetics to *men*, because God put Adam into a deep sleep when He extracted his rib. But male ecclesiastics remained unconvinced as regards the sufferings of *women*, at any rate in childbirth. (R. S., page 105.)

The conception of purpose is a natural one to apply to a human artificer. A man who desires a house cannot, except in the Arabian Nights, have it rise before him as a result of his mere wish; time and labour must be expended before his wish can be gratified. But Omnipotence is subject to no such limitations. If God really thinks well of the human race—an unplausible hypothesis, as it seems to me—why not proceed, as in Genesis, to create man at once? What was the point of the ichthyosaurs, dinosaurs, diplodochi, mastodons, and so on? Dr. Barnes himself confesses, somewhere, that the purpose of the tapeworm is a mystery. What useful purpose is served by rabies and hydrophobia? It is no answer to say that the laws of nature inevitably produce evil as well as good, for God decreed the laws of nature. The evil which is due to sin may be explained as the result of our free will, but the problem of evil in the pre-human world remains. I hardly think Dr. Barnes will accept the solution offered by William Gillespie, that the bodies of beasts of prey were inhabited by devils, whose first sins antedated the brute creation; yet it is difficult to see what other logically satisfying answer can be suggested. The difficulty is old, but none the less real. An omnipotent Being who created a world containing evil not due to sin must Himself be at least partially evil. (R. S., pages 193–4.)

The Greek Church is blamed for denying the double procession of the Holy Ghost and the supremacy of the Pope. We are warned that, although Christ was conceived of the Holy Ghost, we must not suppose that He was the son of the Holy Ghost according to the flesh. (H. W. P., pages 460–461.)

Belief in God and a future life makes it possible to go through life with less of stoic courage than is needed by sceptics. A great many young people lose faith in these dogmas at an age at which despair is easy, and thus have to face a much more intense unhappiness than that which falls to the lot of those who have never had a religious upbringing. Christianity offers reasons for not fearing death or the universe, and in so doing it fails to teach adequately the virtue of courage. The craving for religious faith being largely an outcome of fear, the advocates of faith tend to think that certain kinds of fear are not to be deprecated. In this, to my mind, they are gravely mistaken. To allow oneself to entertain pleasant beliefs as a means of avoiding fear is not to live in the best way. In so far as religion makes its appeal to fear, it is lowering to human dignity. (E. S. O., page 112.)

The whole conception of God is a conception derived from the ancient Oriental despotisms. It is a conception quite unworthy of free men. When you hear people in church debasing themselves and saying that they are miserable sinners, and all the rest of it, it seems contemptible and not worthy of self-respecting human beings. We ought to stand up and look the world frankly in the face. We ought to make the best we can of the world, and if it is not so good as we wish, after all it will still be better than what these others have made of it in all these ages. A good world needs knowledge, kindliness, and courage; it does not need a regretful hankering after the past, or a fettering of the free intelligence by the words uttered long ago by ignorant men. (w. n. c., page 23.)

Religion is based, I think, primarily and mainly upon fear. It is partly the terror of the unknown, and partly the wish to feel that you have a kind of elder brother who will stand by you in all your troubles and disputes. Fear is the basis of the whole thing—fear of the mysterious, fear of defeat, fear of death. . . . Science can help us to get over this craven fear in which mankind has lived for so many generations. Science can teach us, and I think our own hearts can teach us, no longer to look round for imaginary supports, no longer to invent allies in the sky, but rather to look to our own efforts here below to make this world a fit place to live in, instead of the sort of place that the Churches in all these centuries have made it. (w. n. c., page 22.)

Owing to their miraculous powers, priests (in the eleventh century) could determine whether a man should spend eternity in heaven or in hell. If he died while excommunicate, he went to hell; if he died after priests had performed all the proper ceremonies, he would ultimately go to heaven provided he had duly repented and confessed. Before going to heaven, however, he would have to spend some time—perhaps a very long time—suffering the pains of purgatory. Priests could shorten this time by saying masses for his soul, which they were willing to do for a suitable money payment. (H. W. P., page 408.)

Sir James Jeans considers it very doubtful whether, at the present time, there is life anywhere else. Before the Copernican revolution, it was natural to suppose that God's purposes were specially concerned with the earth, but now this has become an unplausible hypothesis. If it is the purpose of the Cosmos to evolve mind, we must regard it as rather incompetent in having produced so little in such a long time. . . . If we accept the rather curious view that the Cosmic Purpose is specially concerned with our little planet, we still find that there is reason to doubt whether it intends quite what the theologians say it does. The earth (unless we use enough poison gas to destroy all life) is likely to remain habitable for some considerable time, but not for ever. Perhaps our atmosphere will gradually fly off into space; perhaps the tides will cause the earth to turn always the same face to the sun, so that one hemisphere will be too hot and the other too cold; perhaps (as in a moral tale by J. B. S. Haldane) the moon will tumble into the earth. If none of these things happen first, we shall in any case be all destroyed when the sun explodes and becomes a cold white dwarf, which, we are told by Jeans, is to happen in about a million million years, though the exact date is still somewhat uncertain.

A million million years gives us some time to prepare for the end, and we may hope that in the meantime both astronomy and gunnery will have made considerable progress. The astronomers may have discovered another star with habitable planets, and the gunners may be able to fire us off to it with a speed approaching that of light, in which case, if the passengers were all young to begin with, some might arrive before dying of old age. It is perhaps a slender hope, but let us make the best of it. (R.S., pages 216, 217, 218.)

I do not believe that a decay of dogmatic belief can do anything but good. I admit at once that new systems of dogma, such as those of the Nazis and the Communists, are even worse than the old systems, but they could never have acquired a hold over men's minds if orthodox dogmatic habits had not been instilled in youth. Stalin's language is full of reminiscences of the theological seminary in which he received his training. What the world needs is not dogma, but an attitude of scientific inquiry, combined with a belief that the torture of millions is not desirable, whether inflicted by Stalin or by a Deity imagined in the likeness of the believer. (H. S. E. P., page 221.)

For four and a half months in 1918 I was in prison for pacifist propaganda; but, by the intervention of Arthur Balfour, I was placed in the first division, so that while in prison I was able to read and write as much as I liked, provided I did no pacifist propaganda. I found prison in many ways quite agreeable. I had no engagements, no difficult decisions to make, no fear of callers, no interruptions to my work. I read enormously; I wrote a book, *Introduction to Mathematical Philosophy*, and began the work for *Analysis of Mind*. I was rather interested in my fellow prisoners, who seemed to me in no way morally inferior to the rest of the population, though they were on the whole slightly below the usual level of intelligence, as was shown by their having been caught. For anybody not in the first division, especially for a person accustomed to reading and writing, prison is a severe and terrible punishment; but for me, thanks to Arthur Balfour, this was not so. I was much cheered on my arrival by the warder at the gate, who had to take particulars about me. He asked my religion, and I replied 'agnostic.' He asked how to spell it, and remarked with a sigh: 'Well, there are many religions, but I suppose they all worship the same God.' This remark kept me cheerful for about a week. (P. F. M., page 30.)

The most influential school of philosophy in Britain at the present day maintains a certain linguistic doctrine to which I am unable to subscribe. I do not wish to misrepresent this school, but I suppose any opponent of any doctrine is thought to misrepresent it by those who hold it. The doctrine, as I understand it, consists in maintaining that the language of daily life, with words used in their ordinary meanings, suffices for philosophy, which has no need of technical terms or of changes in the signification of common terms. I find myself totally unable to accept this view. . . .

Orthodox Christianity asserts that we survive death. What does it mean by this assertion? And in what sense, if any, is the assertion true? The philosophers with whom I am concerned will consider the first of these questions, but will say that the second is none of their business. I agree entirely that, in this case, a discussion as to what is meant is important and highly necessary as a preliminary to a consideration of the substantial question, but if nothing can be said on the substantial question, it seems a waste of time to discuss what it means. These philosophers remind me of the shopkeeper of whom I once asked the shortest way to Winchester. He called to a man in the back premises:

'Gentleman wants to know the shortest way to Winchester.'

'Winchester?' an unseen voice replied.

'Aye.'

'Way to Winchester?'

'Aye.'

'Shortest way?'

'Aye.'

'Dunno.'

He wanted to get the nature of the question clear, but took no interest in answering it. This is exactly what modern philosophy does for the earnest seeker after truth. Is it surprising that young people turn to other studies? (P. F. M., pages 166, 169–170.)

III

SEX AND MARRIAGE

LORD RUSSELL'S VIEWS on marriage and the problems of sex have been subject to bitter controversy, especially in the United States. Criticism has been centred chiefly upon his refusal to sanction ancient sexual tabus. In an age, such as the present, when conformity is virtue, dissent is often confused with subversion. The very mention of Lord Russell's name in connection with sexual ethics has caused hatred in the minds of the more stereotyped. Sex and sin are synonymous terms for those who view life in the light of superstitious moral codes. It can scarcely be denied that until recent years any scientific occupation with sex had been considered wicked.

Lord Russell's book, *Marriage and Morals*, created such a storm of protest that he was legally deprived of a professorship at the City College of New York in 1940. It was thought, by those in power, that any one who would write such a book was unfit to teach. Similar reactions occurred elsewhere, and for a time he was subject to an almost complete boycott throughout the United States. Few books have been subject to such violent controversy. Part of this controversy stems from the fact that most people like to believe themselves more rational than they actually are. If married persons find themselves incompatible, the opponents of reason seem to think that they should go on comfortably thinking themselves in a state of marital bliss.

Lord Russell feels that this is an outcome of tabu morality.

Some of the selections in this chapter are taken from *Marriage and Morals* and show Lord Russell at his wittiest. The humour displayed in the pages which follow is not intended, however, to be amusing for its own sake. *Naïveté* is one thing, wisdom is another; it is hoped that readers will bear this difference in mind.

It is odd that neither the Church nor modern public opinion condemns petting, provided it stops short at a certain point. At what point sin begins is a matter as to which casuists differ. One eminently orthodox Catholic divine laid it down that a confessor may fondle a nun's breasts, provided he does it without evil intent. But I doubt whether modern authorities would agree with him on this point. (U. E., page 80.)

The phrase 'in the sight of God' puzzles me. One would suppose that God sees everything, but apparently this is a mistake. He does not see Reno, for you cannot be divorced in the sight of God. Register offices are a doubtful point. I notice that respectable people, who would not call on anybody who lives in open sin, are quite willing to call on people who have had only a civil marriage; so apparently God does see register offices. (U. E., page 79.)

Tolstoy and Mahatma Gandhi, in their old age, laid it down that *all* sexual intercourse is wicked, even in marriage and with a view to offspring. The Manicheans thought likewise, relying upon men's native sinfulness to supply them with a continually fresh crop of disciples. This doctrine, however, is heretical, though it is equally heretical to maintain that marriage is as praiseworthy as celibacy. Tolstoy thinks tobacco almost as bad as sex; in one of his novels, a man who is contemplating murder smokes a cigarette first in order to generate the necessary homicidal fury. Tobacco, however, is not prohibited in the Scriptures, though,

48

as Samuel Butler points out, St. Paul would no doubt have denounced it if he had known of it. (U. E., pages 79–80.)

[According to St. Thomas] *Divine Law* directs us to love God; also, in a lesser degree, our neighbour. It forbids fornication, because the father should stay with the mother while the children are being reared. It forbids birth control, as being against nature; it does not, however, on this account forbid life-long celibacy. Matrimony should be indissoluble, because the father is needed in the education of the children, both as more rational than the mother, and as having more physical strength when punishment is required. Not all carnal intercourse is sinful, since it is natural; but to think the married state as good as continence is to fall into the heresy of Jovinian. There must be strict monogamy; polygyny is unfair to women, and polyandry makes paternity uncertain. Incest is to be forbidden because it would complicate family life. Against brother-sister incest there is a very curious argument: that if the love of husband and wife were combined with that of brother and sister, mutual attraction would be so strong as to cause unduly frequent intercourse. (H. W. P., page 459.)

St. Paul's views were emphasized and exaggerated by the early Church; celibacy was considered holy and men retired into the desert to wrestle with Satan while he filled their imaginations with lustful visions. (M. M., page 48.)

If the old morality is to be re-established, certain things are essential; some of them are already done, but experience shows that these alone are not effective. The first essential is that the education of girls should be such as to make them stupid and superstitious and ignorant; this requisite is already fulfilled in schools over which the churches have any control. The next requisite is a very severe censorship upon all books giving information on sex subjects; this condition also is coming to be fulfilled in England and in America, since the censorship, without change in the law, is being tightened up by the increasing zeal of the police. These conditions, however, since they exist already, are clearly insufficient. The only thing that will suffice is to remove from young women all opportunity of being alone with men: girls must be forbidden to earn their living by work outside the home; they must never be allowed an outing unless accompanied by their mother or an aunt; the regrettable practice of going to dances without a chaperon must be sternly stamped out. It must be illegal for an unmarried woman under fifty to possess a motor-car, and perhaps it would be wise to subject all unmarried women once a month to medical examination by police doctors, and to send to a penitentiary all such as were found to be not virgins. The use of contraceptives must, of course, be eradicated, and it must be illegal in conversation with unmarried women to throw doubt upon the dogma of eternal damnation. These measures, if carried out vigorously for a hundred years or more, may perhaps do something to stem the rising tide of immorality. I think, however, that in order to avoid the risk of certain abuses, it would be necessary that all policemen and all medical men should be castrated. Perhaps it would be wise to carry this policy a step further, in view of the inherent depravity of the male character. I am inclined to think that moralists would be well advised to advocate that all men should be castrated, with the exception of ministers of religion. Since reading

Elmer Gantry, I have begun to feel that even this exception is perhaps not quite wise. (M. M., pages 90–91.)

Christianity, and more particularly St. Paul, introduced an entirely novel view of marriage, that it existed not primarily for the procreation of children, but to prevent the sin of fornication. . . . (I Cor. vii. 1–9.)

St. Paul makes no mention whatever of children; the biological purpose of marriage appears to him wholly unimportant. This is quite natural, since he imagined that the Second Coming was imminent and that the world would soon come to an end. At the Second Coming men were to be divided into sheep and goats, and the only thing of real importance was to find oneself among the sheep on that occasion. St. Paul holds that sexual intercourse, even in marriage, is something of a handicap in the attempt to win salvation (I Cor. vii. 32–4). Nevertheless it is possible for married people to be saved, but fornication is deadly sin, and the unrepentant fornicator is sure to find himself among the goats. I remember once being advised by a doctor to abandon the practice of smoking, and he said that I should find it easier if, whenever the desire came upon me, I proceeded to suck an acid drop. It is in this spirit that St. Paul recommends marriage. He does not suggest that it is quite as pleasant as fornication, but he thinks it may enable the weaker brethren to withstand temptation; he does not suggest for a moment that there may be any positive good in marriage, or that affection between husband and wife may be a beautiful and desirable thing, nor does he take the slightest interest in the family; fornication holds the centre of the stage in his thoughts, and the whole of his sexual ethics is arranged with reference to it. It is just as if one were to maintain that the sole reason for baking bread is to prevent people from stealing cake. (M. M., pages 44, 45, 46, 47.)

The Puritans, in their determination to avoid the pleasures of sex, became somewhat more conscious than people had been before of the pleasures of the table. As a seventeenth-century critic of Puritanism says:

> *Would you enjoy gay nights and pleasant dinners?*
> *Then must you board with saints and bed with sinners.*

It would seem, therefore, that the Puritans did not succeed in subduing the purely corporeal part of our human nature, since what they took away from sex they added to gluttony. Gluttony is regarded by the Catholic Church as one of the seven deadly sins, and those who practise it are placed by Dante in one of the deeper circles of hell, but it is a somewhat vague sin, since it is hard to say where a legitimate interest in food ceases, and guilt begins to be incurred. Is it wicked to eat anything that is not nourishing? If so, with every salted almond we risk damnation. (M. M., page 290.)

Men have from time immemorial been allowed in practice, if not in theory, to indulge in illicit sexual relations. It has not been expected of a man that he should be a virgin on entering marriage, and even after marriage, infidelities are not viewed very gravely if they never come to the knowledge of a man's wife and neighbours. The possibility of this system has depended upon prostitution. This institution, however, is one which it is difficult for a modern to defend, and few will suggest that women should acquire the same rights as men through the establishment of a class of male prostitutes for the satisfaction of women who wish, like their husbands, to seem virtuous without being so. . . . Every conventional moralist who takes the trouble to think it out will see that he is committed in practice to what is called the double standard, that is to say, the view that sexual virtue is more essential in a woman than in a man. It is all very well to argue that his theoretical ethic demands continence of men also. To this there is the obvious retort that the demand cannot be enforced on the men since it is easy for them to sin secretly. The conventional moralist is thus committed against his will not only to an inequality as between men and women, but also to the view that it is better for a young man to have intercourse with prostitutes than with girls of his own class, in spite of the fact that with the latter, though not with the former, his relations are not mercenary and may be affectionate and altogether delightful. Moralists, of course, do not think out the consequences of advocating a morality which they know will not be obeyed; they think that so long as they do not advocate prostitution they are not responsible for the fact that prostitution is the inevitable outcome of their teaching. This, however, is only another illustration of the well-known fact that the professional moralist in our day is a man of less than average intelligence. (M. M., pages 86, 87, 88.)

The Catholic Church has not remained so unbiological as St. Paul and the hermits of the Thebaid. From St. Paul one gathers that marriage is to be regarded solely as a more or less legitimate outlet for lust. One would not gather from his words that he would have any objection to birth control: on the contrary, one would be led to suppose that he would regard as dangerous the periods of continence involved in pregnancy and childbirth. The Church has taken a different view. Marriage in the orthodox Christian doctrine has two purposes: one, that recognized by St. Paul, the other, the procreation of children. The consequence has been to make sexual morality even more difficult than it was made by St. Paul. Not only is sexual intercourse only legitimate within marriage, but even between husband and wife it becomes a sin unless it is hoped that it will lead to pregnancy. The desire for legitimate offspring is, in fact, according to the Catholic Church, the only motive which can justify sexual intercourse. But this motive always justifies it, no matter what cruelty may accompany it. If the wife hates sexual intercourse, if she is likely to die of another pregnancy, if the child is likely to be diseased or insane, if there is not enough money to prevent the utmost extreme of misery, that does not prevent the man from being justified in insisting on his conjugal rights, provided only that he hopes to beget a child. (M. M., pages 52–53.)

The view of the orthodox moralist (this includes the police and the magistrates, but hardly any modern educators) on the question of sex knowledge may, I fancy, be fairly stated as follows. . . . There is no doubt that sexual misconduct is promoted by sexual thoughts, and that the best road to virtue is to keep the young occupied in mind and body with matters wholly unconnected with sex. They must, therefore, be told nothing whatever about sex; they must as far as possible be prevented from talking about it with each other, and grownups must pretend that there is no such topic. It is possible by these means to keep a girl in ignorance until the night of her marriage, when it is to be expected that the facts will so shock her as to produce exactly that attitude towards sex which every sound moralist considers desirable in women. (M. M., pages 98–99.)

Catholic teaching . . . has a two-fold basis; it rests, on the one hand, upon the asceticism which we already find in St. Paul, on the other, upon the view that it is good to bring into the world as many souls as possible, since every soul is capable of salvation. For some reason which I do not understand, the fact that souls are equally capable of damnation is not taken into account, and yet it seems quite as relevant. Catholics, for example, use their political influence to prevent Protestants from practising birth control, and yet they must hold that the great majority of Protestant children whom their political action causes to exist will endure eternal torment in the next world. This makes their action seem somewhat unkind, but doubtless these are mysteries which the profane cannot hope to understand. (M. M., pages 53–54.)

Within the monogamic family there are many varieties. Marriages may be decided by the parties themselves or by their parents. In some countries the bride is purchased; in others, e.g. France, the bridegroom. Then there may be all kinds of differences as regards divorce, from the Catholic extreme, which permits no divorce, to the law of old China, which permitted a man to divorce his wife for being a chatterbox. Constancy or quasi-constancy in sex relations arises among animals, as well as among human beings, where, for the preservation of the species, the participation of the male is necessary for the rearing of the young. Birds, for example, have to sit upon their eggs continuously to keep them warm, and also have to spend a good many hours of the day getting food. To do both is, among many species, impossible for one bird, and therefore male co-operation is essential. The consequence is that most birds are models of virtue. Among human beings the co-operation of the father is a great biological advantage to the offspring, especially in unsettled times and among turbulent populations; but with the growth of modern civilization the role of the father is being increasingly taken over by the State, and there is reason to think that a father may cease before long to be biologically advantageous, at any rate in the wage-earning class. If this should occur, we must expect a complete breakdown of traditional morality, since there will no longer be any reason why a mother should wish the paternity of her child to be indubitable. Plato would have us go a step further, and put the State not only in place of the father but in that of the mother also. I am not myself sufficiently an admirer of the State, or sufficiently impressed with the delights of orphan asylums, to be enthusiastic in favour of this scheme. (M. M., pages 13–14.)

Malinowski found it quite impossible, in spite of his best argumentative efforts, to persuade his friends on the islands that there is such a thing as paternity. They regarded this as a silly story invented by the missionaries. Christianity is a patriarchal religion, and cannot be made emotionally or intellectually intelligible to people who do not recognize fatherhood. Instead of 'God the Father' it would be necessary to speak of 'God the Maternal Uncle,' but this does not give quite the right shade of meaning, since fatherhood implies both power and love, whereas in Melanesia the maternal uncle has the power and the father has the love. The idea that men are God's children is one which cannot be conveyed to the Trobriand Islanders, since they do not think that anybody is the child of any male. Consequently, missionaries are compelled to tackle first the facts of physiology before they can go on to preach their religion. One gathers from Malinowksi that they have had no success in this initial task, and have, therefore, been quite unable to proceed to the teaching of the Gospel. (M. M., pages 21–22.)

Cruelty is in theory a perfectly adequate ground for divorce, but it may be interpreted so as to become absurd. When the most eminent of all film stars was divorced by his wife for cruelty, one of the counts in the proof of cruelty was that he used to bring home friends who talked about Kant. I can hardly suppose that it was the intention of the California legislators to enable any woman to divorce her husband on the ground that he was sometimes guilty of intelligent conversation in her presence. (M. M., page 234.)

The need for prostitution arises from the fact that many men are either unmarried or away from their wives on journeys, that such men are not content to remain continent, and that in a conventionally virtuous community they do not find respectable women available. Society therefore sets apart a certain class of women for the satisfaction of those masculine needs which it is ashamed to acknowledge yet afraid to leave wholly unsatisfied. The prostitute has the advantage, not only that she is available at a moment's notice, but that, having no life outside her profession, she can remain hidden without difficulty, and the man who has been with her can return to his wife, his family, and his church with unimpaired dignity. She, however, poor woman, in spite of the undoubted service she performs, in spite of the fact that she safeguards the virtues of wives and daughters and the apparent virtue of church-wardens, is universally despised, thought to be an outcast, and not allowed to associate with ordinary people except in the way of business. This blazing injustice began with the victory of the Christian religion, and has been continued ever since. (M. M., page 146.)

Missionaries may argue that the superiority of the Christian code is known by revelation. The philoso-

pher, however, must observe that other religions make
the same claim . . . the Manicheans thought it wicked
to eat any animal food except fish, but many sects have
considered this exception an abomination. The Du-
khobors refused military service, but held it proper to
dance naked all together round a camp fire; being
persecuted for the former tenet in Russia, they emi-
grated to Canada, where they were persecuted for the
latter. The Mormons had a divine revelation in favour
of polygamy, but under pressure from the United
States Government they discovered that the revelation
was not binding. (H. S. E. P., pages 45–6.)

The recognition of children as one of the purposes of
marriage is very partial in Catholic doctrine. It ex-
hausts itself in drawing the inference that intercourse
not intended to lead to children is sin. It has never gone
so far as to permit the dissolution of a marriage on the
ground of sterility. However ardently a man may desire children, if it happens that his wife is barren, he
has no remedy in Christian ethics. The fact is that the
positive purpose of marriage, namely procreation,
plays a very subordinate part, and its main purpose
remains, as with St. Paul, the prevention of sin. Fornication still holds the centre of the stage, and marriage
is still regarded essentially as a somewhat less regrettable alternative. (M. M., page 54.)

It is permissible with certain precautions to speak in
print of *coitus*, but it is not permissible to employ the
monosyllabic synonym for this word. This has recently been decided in the case of *Sleeveless Errand*.
Sometimes this prohibition of simple language has
grave consequences; for example, Mrs. Sanger's pamphlet on birth control, which is addressed to working
women, was declared obscene on the ground that

working women could understand it. Dr. Marie Stopes's books, on the other hand, are not illegal, because their language can only be understood by persons with a certain amount of education. The consequence is that, while it is permissible to teach birth control to the well-to-do, it is criminate to teach it to wage-earners and their wives. I commend this fact to the notice of the Eugenic Society, which is perpetually bewailing the fact that wage-earners breed faster than middle-class people, while carefully abstaining from any attempt to change the state of the law which is the cause of this fact. (M. M., pages 111–112.)

The commonest objection to birth control is that it is against 'nature.' (For some reason we are not allowed to say that celibacy is against nature; the only reason I can think of is that it is not new.) Malthus saw only three ways of keeping down the population: moral restraint, vice, and misery. Moral restraint, he admitted, was not likely to be practised on a large scale. 'Vice,' i.e., birth control, he, as a clergyman, viewed with abhorrence. There remained misery. In his comfortable parsonage, he contemplated the misery of the great majority of mankind with equanimity, and pointed out the fallacies of the reformers who hoped to alleviate it. (U. E., page 100.)

Very few men or women who have had a conventional upbringing have learnt to feel decently about sex and marriage. Their education has taught them that deceitfulness and lying are considered virtues by parents and teachers; that sexual relations, even within marriage, are more or less disgusting, and that in propagating the species men are yielding to their animal nature while women are submitting to a painful duty. This attitude has made marriage unsatisfying both to men and to women, and the lack of instinctive satisfaction has turned to cruelty masquerading as morality. (M. M., page 98.)

A boy should be taught that in no circumstances is conversation on sexual subjects permissible, not even in marriage. This increases the likelihood that when he marries he will give his wife a disgust of sex and thus preserve her from the risk of adultery. Sex outside marriage is sin; sex within marriage is not sin, since it is necessary to the propagation of the human species, but is a disagreeable duty imposed on man as a punishment for the Fall, and to be undertaken in the same spirit in which one submits to a surgical operation. Unfortunately, unless great pains are taken, the sexual act tends to be associated with pleasure, but by sufficient moral care this can be prevented, at any rate in the female. It is illegal in England to state in print that a wife can and should derive sexual pleasure from intercourse. (I have myself heard a pamphlet condemned as obscene in a court of law on this among other grounds.) It is on the above outlook in regard to sex that the attitude of the law, the Church, and the old-fashioned educators of the young is based. (M. M., page 100.)

Sex relations as a dignified, rational, wholehearted activity in which the complete personality co-operates, do not often, I think, occur in America outside marriage. To this extent the moralists have been successful. They have not prevented fornication; on the contrary, if anything, their opposition, by making it spicy, has made it more common. But they have succeeded in making it almost as undesirable as they say it is, just as they have succeeded in making much of the alcohol consumed as poisonous as they assert all alcohol to be. They have compelled young people to take sex neat, divorced from daily companionship, from a common work, and from all psychological intimacy. The more timid of the young do not go so far as complete sexual relations, but content themselves with producing prolonged states of sexual excitement without satisfaction, which are nervously debilitating, and calculated to make the full enjoyment of sex at a later date difficult or impossible. (M. M., page 159.)

Most men and women, given suitable conditions, will feel passionate love at some period of their lives. For the inexperienced, however, it is very difficult to distinguish passionate love from mere sex hunger; especially is this the case with well-brought-up girls, who have been taught that they could not possibly like to kiss a man unless they loved him. If a girl is expected to be a virgin when she marries, it will very often happen that she is trapped by a transient and trivial sex attraction, which a woman with sexual experience could easily distinguish from love. This has undoubtedly been a frequent cause of unhappy marriages. Even where mutual love exists, it may be poisoned by the belief of one or both that it is sinful. This belief may, of course, be well founded. Parnell, for example, undoubtedly sinned in committing adultery, since he thereby postponed the fulfilment of the hopes of Ireland for many years. (M. M., pages 123–124.)

Peasant children early become accustomed to what are called the facts of life, which they can observe not only among human beings but among animals. They are thus saved from both ignorance and fastidiousness. The carefully educated children of the well-to-do, on the contrary, are shielded from all practical knowledge of sexual matters, and even the most modern parents, who teach children out of books, do not give them that sense of practical familiarity which the peasant child early acquires. The triumph of Christian teaching is when a man and woman marry without either having had previous sexual experience. (M. M., pages 137–138.)

IV

EDUCATION

ALTHOUGH LORD RUSSELL'S CONTRIBUTIONS to education have not been as titanic or promethean as his contributions to mathematics and philosophy, the impact of his views on education has been considerable. He is an ardent leader of those who insist that education ought to emphasize scientific methods of inquiry rather than the transmission of a settled body of knowledge. He refuses to compromise with those who adopt persecution, censorship, and other controls over education.

Lord Russell has had wide personal experience with a variety of educational problems. From 1927 to 1932 he and his wife, Dora Winifred Black, directed the activities of an experimental school for young children. Since 1900 he has lectured widely in England, America, and the Far East at such notable institutions as Cambridge University, England; the University of Chicago, the University of California, and Harvard University in the United States; and the National University in Peking, China. He has also been prevented from accepting a number of other professorial engagements because he advocated 'dangerous' ideas. He has been called an enemy of religion and morality by those who prefer that educators instil dogmatic creeds, instead of a spirit of critical inquiry.

During the present century considerable attention has been focused upon the more desirable values of education—the developing of scientific attitudes and the forming of mental habits which lead to sound judgments. To these, however, much as enlightened educators may regret it, most students react with indifference. What they really value from the education to which they are exposed are final *answers* to problems. The thought that objective methods of inquiry are more valid than fixed answers to problems rarely occurs to the stereotyped mind. What is needed in education are not systems of dogma, but rather an attitude of scientific inquiry. Students ought to be taught to base their beliefs upon observation and inference as impersonal and as much devoid of dogmatic bias as is possible for human beings.

The flashes of wit that Lord Russell displays in the selections which follow point up the struggle between those who advocate inflexible doctrines and those who advocate freedom in education. The former are largely responsible for planting seeds of fear, hate, and intolerance in the minds of the young which often blossom into full-scale persecution crusades. History records numerous instances of the dreadful consequences of this kind of education. Hitler's Germany is a case in point. There are other undesirable results of this educational method. Science, for example, remained static until a few brave men challenged the opinions of ancient authorities. Before 1500 anyone who dared disagree with the official opinion of the Church or State was silenced.

It is only in a spirit of free inquiry that desirable learning can take place. In this kind of atmosphere students are not compelled to believe in tenets, but only in evidence which is objective. The substitution of evidence for dogma, as a basis for belief, is one of the great achievements that science has conferred upon mankind. Lord Russell refuses to surrender to the pressures of those who insist upon less than a scientific attitude in education.

Man, it would seem, has descended from arboreal apes. They lived a happy life in tropical forests, eating coconuts when they were hungry, and throwing them at each other when they were not. They were perpetually occupied in gymnastics, and acquired an agility which to us is truly astonishing. But after some millions of years of this arboreal paradise, their numbers increased to the point where the supply of coconuts was no longer adequate. The population problem set in, and was dealt with in two different ways: those who lived in the middle of the forest learned to throw coconuts with such accuracy as to disable adversaries, whose consequent death relieved the pressure of population, but those who lived on the edge of the forest found another method: they looked out over the fields and discovered that they yielded delicious fruits of various kinds quite as pleasant as coconuts, and gradually they came down from the trees and spent more and more time in the open on the ground . . . they soon discovered that if you live on the ground it is easy to pick up stones, which are more effective missiles than coconuts. (N. H. C. W., page 16.)

I am not myself in any degree ashamed of having changed my opinions. What physicist who was already active in 1900 would dream of boasting that his opinions had not changed during the last half century? In science men change their opinions when new knowledge becomes available, but philosophy in the minds of many is assimilated rather to theology than to science. A theologian proclaims eternal truths, the creeds remain unchanged since the Council of Nicaea. Where nobody knows anything, there is no point in changing your mind. (D. M. M. M., preface.)

Owing to the identification of religion with virtue, together with the fact that the most religious men are not the most intelligent, a religious education gives courage to the stupid to resist the authority of educated men, as has happened, for example, where the teaching of evolution has been made illegal. So far as I can remember, there is not one word in the Gospels in praise of intelligence; and in this respect ministers of religion follow gospel authority more closely than in some others. (E. S. O., pages 114–15.)

If you think that your belief is based upon reason, you will support it by argument, rather than by persecution, and will abandon it if the argument goes against you. But if your belief is based on faith, you will realize that argument is useless, and will therefore resort to force either in the form of persecution or by stunting and distorting the minds of the young in what is called 'education.' This last is peculiarly dastardly, since it takes advantage of the defencelessness of immature minds. Unfortunately it is practised in a greater or less degree in the schools of every civilized country. (H. S. E. P., pages 220–221.)

Punctuality is a quality the need of which is bound up with social co-operation. It has nothing to do with the relation of the soul to God, or with mystic insight, or with any of the matters with which the more elevated and spiritual moralists are concerned. One would be surprised to find a saint getting drunk, but one would not be surprised to find him late for an engagement. And yet in the ordinary business of life punctuality is absolutely necessary. (E. S. O., pages 34–35.)

To modern educated people, it seems obvious that matters of fact are to be ascertained by observation, not by consulting ancient authorities. But this is an entirely modern conception, which hardly existed before the seventeenth century. Aristotle maintained that women have fewer teeth than men; although he was twice married, it never occurred to him to verify this statement by examining his wives' mouths. He said also that children would be healthier if conceived when the wind is in the north. One gathers that the two Mrs. Aristotles both had to run out and look at the weathercock every evening before going to bed. He states that a man bitten by a mad dog will not go mad, but any other animal will (*Hist. Am.*, 704a); that the bite of the shrewmouse is dangerous to horses, especially if the mouse is pregnant (ibid., 604b); that elephants suffering from insomnia can be cured by rubbing their shoulders with salt, olive oil, and warm water (ibid., 605a); and so on and so on. Nevertheless, classical dons, who have never observed any animal except the cat and the dog, continue to praise Aristotle for his fidelity to observation. (I. s. s., page 7.)

It is not altogether true that persuasion is one thing and force is another. Many forms of persuasion—even many of which everybody approves—are really a kind of force. Consider what we do to our children. We do not say to them: 'Some people think the earth is round, and others think it flat; when you grow up, you can, if you like, examine the evidence and form your own conclusion.' Instead of this we say: 'The earth *is* round.' By the time our children are old enough to examine the evidence, our propaganda has closed their minds, and the most persuasive arguments of the Flat Earth Society make no impression. The same applies to the moral precepts that we consider really important, such as 'don't pick your nose' or 'don't eat peas with a knife.' There may, for aught I know, be admirable reasons for eating peas with a knife, but the hypnotic effect of early persuasion has made me completely incapable of appreciating them. (P.: A. N. S. A., pages 268–269.)

In universities, mathematics is taught mainly to men who are going to teach mathematics to men who are going to teach mathematics to. . . . Sometimes, it is true, there is an escape from this treadmill. Archimedes used mathematics to kill Romans, Galileo to improve the Grand Duke of Tuscany's artillery, modern physicists (grown more ambitious) to exterminate the human race. It is usually on this account that the study of mathematics is commended to the general public as worthy of State support. (H. S. E. P., page 54.)

Until the time of Galileo, astronomers, following Aristotle, believed that everything in the heavens, from the moon upwards, is unchanging and incorruptible. Since Laplace, no reputable astronomer has held this view. Nebulae, stars, and planets, we now believe, have all developed gradually. Some stars, for instance the companion of Sirius, are 'dead'; they have at some time undergone a cataclysm which has enormously diminished the amount of light and heat radiating from them. Our own planet, in which philosophers are apt to take a parochial and excessive interest, was once too hot to support life, and will in time be too cold. After ages during which the earth produced harmless trilobites and butterflies, evolution progressed to the point at which it generated Neros, Genghis Khans, and Hitlers. This, however, is a passing nightmare; in time the earth will become again incapable of supporting life, and peace will return. (U. E., pages 8–9.)

Generalizing, we may say that Dr. Dewey, like every-one else, divides beliefs into two classes, of which one is good and the other bad. He holds, however, that a belief may be good at one time and bad at another. . . . A belief about some event in the past is to be classified as 'good' or 'bad,' not according to whether the event really took place, but according to the future effects of the belief. The results are curious. Suppose some-body says to me: 'Did you have coffee with your breakfast this morning?' If I am an ordinary person, I shall try to remember. But if I am a disciple of Dr. Dewey I shall say: 'Wait a while; I must try two ex-periments before I can tell you.' I shall, then, first make myself believe that I had coffee, and observe the conse-quences, if any; I shall then make myself believe that I did not have coffee, and again observe the conse-quences, if any. I shall then compare the two sets of consequences, to see which I found the more satis-factory. If there is a balance on one side I shall decide for that answer. If there is not, I shall have to confess that I cannot answer the question.

But this is not the end of our trouble. How am I to know the consequences of believing that I had coffee for breakfast? If I say 'the consequences are such-and-such,' this in turn will have to be tested by its conse-quences before I can know whether what I have said was a 'good' or a 'bad' statement. And even if this difficulty were overcome, how am I to judge which set of consequences is the more satisfactory? One de-cision as to whether I had coffee may fill me with contentment, the other with determination to further the war effort. Each of these may be considered good, but until I have decided which is better I cannot tell whether I had coffee for breakfast. (H. W. P., page 825.)

The date of the creation of the world (according to the orthodox view) can be inferred from the gene-

alogies in Genesis, which tell how old each patriarch
was when his oldest son was born. Some margin of
controversy was permissible, owing to certain ambi-
guities and to differences between the Septuagint and
the Hebrew text; but in the end Protestant Christen-
dom generally accepted the date 4004 B.C., fixed by
Archbishop Usher. Dr. Lightfoot, Vice-Chancellor of
the University of Cambridge, who accepted this date
for the Creation, thought that a careful study of Genesis made even greater precision possible; the creation
of man, according to him, took place at 9.00 A.M. on
October 23rd. This, however, has never been an article
of faith; you might believe, without risk of heresy,
that Adam and Eve came into existence on October
16th or October 30th, provided your reasons were derived from Genesis. The day of the week was, of
course, known to have been Friday, since God rested
on the Saturday. (R. S., pages 51–2.)

The first German to take notice of Hume was Im-
manuel Kant, who had been content, up to the age of
about forty-five, with the dogmatic tradition derived
from Leibniz. Then, as he says himself, Hume 'awak-
ened him from his dogmatic slumbers.' After meditat-
ing for twelve years, he produced his great work, the
Critique of Pure Reason; seven years later, at the age
of sixty-four, he produced the *Critique of Practical
Reason*, in which he resumed his dogmatic slumbers
after nearly twenty years of uncomfortable wakeful-
ness. (U. E., page 51.)

Children are made to learn bits of Shakespeare by
heart, with the result that ever after they associate him
with pedantic boredom. If they could meet him in the
flesh, full of jollity and ale, they would be astonished,
and if they had never heard of him before they might

be led by his jollity to see what he had written. But if at school they had been inoculated against him, they will never be able to enjoy him. The same sort of thing applies to music lessons. Human beings have certain capacities for spontaneous enjoyment, but moralists and pedants possess themselves of the apparatus of these enjoyments, and having extracted what they consider the poison of pleasure they leave them dreary and dismal and devoid of everything that gives them value. Shakespeare did not write with a view to boring school-children; he wrote with a view to delighting his audiences. If he does not give you delight, you had better ignore him. (N. H. C. W., page 201.)

Fichte laid it down that education should aim at destroying free will, so that, after pupils have left school, they shall be incapable, throughout the rest of their lives, of thinking or acting otherwise than as their schoolmasters would have wished. But in his day this was an unattainable ideal. What he regarded as the best system in existence produced Karl Marx. In future such failures are not likely to occur where there is dictatorship. Diet, injections, and injunctions will combine, from a very early age, to produce the sort of character and the sort of beliefs that the authorities consider desirable, and any serious criticism of the powers that be will become psychologically impossible. Even if all are miserable, all will believe themselves happy, because the government will tell them that they are so. (I. S. S., page 50.)

Boys and young men acquire readily the moral sentiments of their social milieu, whatever these sentiments may be. The boy who has been taught at home that it is wicked to swear, easily loses this belief when he finds that the schoolfellows whom he most admires are addicted to blasphemy. (H. S. E. P., page 76.)

Dread of disaster makes everybody act in the very way that increases the disaster. Psychologically the situation is analogous to that of people trampled to death when there is a panic in a theatre caused by a cry of 'Fire!' In the situation that existed in the great depression, things could only be set right by causing the idle plant to work again. But everybody felt that to do so was to risk almost certain loss. Within the framework of classical economics there was no solution. Roosevelt saved the situation by bold and heretical action. He spent billions of public money and created a huge public debt, but by so doing he revived production and brought his country out of the depression. Businessmen, who in spite of such a sharp lesson continued to believe in old-fashioned economics, were infinitely shocked, and although Roosevelt saved them from ruin, they continued to curse him and to speak of him as 'the madman in the White House.' Except for Fabre's investigation of the behaviour of insects, I do not know any equally striking example of inability to learn from experience. (N. H. C. W., pages 132–133.)

You may, if you are an old-fashioned schoolmaster, wish to consider yourself full of universal benevolence, and at the same time derive great pleasure from caning boys. In order to reconcile these two desires you have to persuade yourself that caning has a reformatory influence. If a psychiatrist tells you that it has no such influence on some peculiarly irritating class of young sinners, you will fly into a rage and accuse him of being coldly intellectual. There is a splendid example of this pattern in the furious diatribe of the great Dr. Arnold of Rugby against those who thought ill of flogging. (H. S. E. P., preface, page 9.)

Until very recently, it was universally believed that men are congenitally more intelligent than women;

even so enlightened a man as Spinoza decides against votes for women on this ground. Among white men, it is held that white men are by nature superior to men of other colours, and especially to black men; in Japan, on the contrary, it is thought that yellow is the best colour. In Haiti, when they make statues of Christ and Satan, they make Christ black and Satan white. Aristotle and Plato considered Greeks so innately superior to barbarians that slavery is justified so long as the master is Greek and the slave barbarian. (U. E., page 88.)

Male superiority in former days was easily demonstrated, because if a woman questioned her husband's he could beat her. From superiority in this respect others were thought to follow. Men were more reasonable than women, more inventive, less swayed by their emotions, and so on. Anatomists, until the women had the vote, developed a number of ingenious arguments from the study of the brain to show that men's intellectual capacities must be greater than women's. Each of these arguments in turn was proved to be fallacious, but it always gave place to another from which the same conclusion would follow. It used to be held that the male foetus acquires a soul after six weeks, but the female only after three months. This opinion also has been abandoned since women have had the vote. Thomas Aquinas states parenthetically, as something entirely obvious, that men are more rational than women. For my part, I see no evidence of this. (U. E., page 158.)

Some 'advanced Thinkers' are of opinion that anyone who differs from the conventional opinion must be in the right. This is a delusion; if it were not, truth would be easier to come by than it is. There are infinite possi-

bilities of error, and more cranks take up unfashionable
errors than unfashionable truths. I met once an electri-
cal engineer whose first words to me were: 'How do
you do? There are two methods of faith-healing, the
one practised by Christ and the one practised by most
Christian Scientists. I practise the method practised by
Christ.' Shortly afterwards, he was sent to prison for
making out fraudulent balance-sheets. The law does
not look kindly on the intrusion of faith into this
region. (U. E., page 96.)

I knew an eminent lunacy doctor who took to
philosophy, and taught a new logic which, as he
frankly confessed, he had learned from his lunatics.
When he died he left a will founding a professorship
for the teaching of his new scientific methods, but unfortunately he left no assets. Arithmetic proved re-
calcitrant to lunatic logic. On one occasion a man came
to ask me to recommend some of my books, as he was
interested in philosophy. I did so, but he returned next
day saying that he had been reading one of them, and
had found only one statement he could understand,
and that one seemed to him false. I asked him what it
was, and he said it was the statement that Julius Caesar
is dead. When I asked him why he did not agree, he
drew himself up and said: 'Because I am Julius Caesar.'
(U. E., page 96.)

The demand for certainty is one which is natural to
man, but is nevertheless an intellectual vice. If you take
your children for a picnic on a doubtful day, they will
demand a dogmatic answer as to whether it will be
fine or wet, and be disappointed in you when you
cannot be sure. The same sort of assurance is de-
manded, in later life, of those who undertake to lead

populations into the Promised Land. 'Liquidate the capitalists and the survivors will enjoy eternal bliss.' 'Exterminate the Jews and everyone will be virtuous.' 'Kill the Croats and let the Serbs reign.' 'Kill the Serbs and let the Croats reign.' These are samples of the slogans that have won wide popular acceptance in our time. Even a modicum of philosophy would make it impossible to accept such bloodthirsty nonsense. But so long as men are not trained to withhold judgment in the absence of evidence, they will be led astray by cocksure prophets, and it is likely that their leaders will be either ignorant fanatics or dishonest charlatans. To endure uncertainty is difficult, but so are most of the other virtues. For the learning of every virtue there is an appropriate discipline, and for the learning of suspended judgment the best discipline is philosophy. (U. E., pages 26–27.)

Those who have a passion for quick returns and for an exact balance sheet of effort and reward may feel impatient of a study which cannot, in the present state of our knowledge, arrive at certainties, and which encourages what may be thought the time-wasting occupation of inconclusive meditation on insoluble problems. To this view I cannot in any degree subscribe. Some kind of philosophy is a necessity to all but the most thoughtless, and in the absence of knowledge it is almost sure to be a silly philosophy. The result of this is that the human race becomes divided into rival groups of fanatics, each group firmly persuaded that its own brand of nonsense is sacred truth, while the other side's is damnable heresy. Arians and Catholics, Crusaders and Moslems, Protestants and adherents of the Pope, Communists, and Fascists, have filled large parts of the last 1,600 years with futile strife, when a little philosophy would have shown both sides in all these disputes that neither had any good reason to believe itself in the right. (U. E., page 26.)

When the journey from means to end is not too long, the means themselves are enjoyed if the end is ardently desired. A boy will toil uphill with a toboggan for the sake of the few brief moments of bliss during the descent; no one has to urge him to be industrious, and however he may puff and pant he is still happy. But if instead of the immediate reward you promised him an old-age pension at seventy, his energy would very quickly flag. (A. I., page 38.)

Herd pressure is to be judged by two things: first, its intensity, and second, its direction. If it is very intense, it produces adults who are timid and conventional, except in a few rare instances. This is regrettable, however excellent may be the moral standards by which the herd is actuated. In *Tom Brown's Schooldays* there is a boy who is kicked for saying his prayers. This book had a great effect, and among my contemporaries I knew one who had been kicked at school for *not* saying his prayers. I regret to say that he remained through life a prominent atheist. (E. S. O., pages 96–7.)

Dr. Arnold, the hero of *Tom Brown's Schooldays*, and the admired reformer of public schools, came across some cranks who thought it a mistake to flog boys. Anyone reading his outburst of furious indignation against this opinion will be forced to the conclusion that he enjoyed inflicting floggings, and did not wish to be deprived of this pleasure. (U. E., pages 147–148.)

Men of science are being increasingly compelled to pursue the ends of governments rather than those proper to science. . . . The scientist who discovers how to injure others is therefore at least as much honoured as the one who shows us how to benefit ourselves. The pursuit of knowledge for its own sake, which was once the purpose of science, is lost sight of; there are even philosophers who tell us that there is no such thing. A physicist who wishes to study uranium can have access to any amount of public money, but if he wished to devote equal skill and equal labour to the study of (say) carbon, he would have to persuade his government that he was on the track of a method of inventing robots. (B. D., September 1948, pages 14–15.)

In the welter of conflicting fanaticisms, one of the few unifying forces is scientific truthfulness, by which I mean the habit of basing our beliefs upon observations and inferences as impersonal, and as much divested of local and temperamental bias as is possible for human beings. To have insisted upon the introduction of this virtue into philosophy, and to have invented a powerful method by which it can be rendered fruitful, are the chief merits of the philosophical school of which I am a member. The habit of careful veracity acquired in the practise of this philosophical method can be extended to the whole sphere of human activity, producing, wherever it exists, a lessening of fanaticism with an increasing capacity of sympathy and mutual understanding. (H. W. P., page 836.)

I was a solitary, shy, priggish youth. I had no experience of the social pleasures of boyhood and did not miss them. But I liked mathematics, and mathematics was suspect because it has no ethical content. I came also to disagree with the theological opinions of my family, and as I grew up I became increasingly interested in philosophy, of which they profoundly

disapproved. Every time the subject came up they repeated with unfailing regularity, 'What is mind? No
matter. What is matter? Never mind.' After some fifty
or sixty repetitions, this remark ceased to amuse me.
(P. F. M., pages 3, 4.)

I think the first thing that led me toward philosophy
(though at that time the word 'philosophy' was still
unknown to me) occurred at the age of eleven. My
childhood was mainly solitary as my only brother
was seven years older than I was. No doubt as a
result of much solitude I became rather solemn, with
a great deal of time for thinking but not much knowledge for my thoughtfulness to exercise itself upon. I
had, though I was not yet aware of it, the pleasure in
demonstrations which is typical of the mathematical
mind. After I grew up I found others who felt as I
did on this matter. My friend G. H. Hardy, who was
professor of pure mathematics, enjoyed this pleasure in
a very high degree. He told me once that if he could
find a proof that I was going to die in five minutes he
would of course be sorry to lose me, but this sorrow
would be quite outweighed by pleasure in the proof.
I entirely sympathized with him and was not at all
offended. Before I began the study of geometry some-
body had told me that it proved things and this caused
me to feel delight when my brother said he would
teach it to me. Geometry in those days was still
'Euclid.' My brother began at the beginning with the
definitions. These I accepted readily enough. But he
came next to the axioms. 'These,' he said, 'can't be
proved, but they have to be assumed before the rest
can be proved.' At these words my hopes crumbled. I
had thought it would be wonderful to find something
that one could *prove*, and then it turned out that this
could only be done by means of assumptions of which

there was no proof. I looked at my brother with a sort of indignation and said: 'But why should I admit these things if they can't be proved?' He replied, 'Well, if you won't, we can't go on.' (P. F. M., pages 14–15.)

There are some simple maxims which I think might be commended to writers of expository prose. First: never use a long word if a short word will do. Second: if you want to make a statement with a great many qualifications, put some of the qualifications in separate sentences. Third: do not let the beginning of your sentence lead the reader to an expectation which is contradicted by the end. Take, say, such a sentence as the following, which might occur in a work on sociology: 'Human beings are completely exempt from undesirable behaviour patterns only when certain prerequisites, not satisfied except in a small percentage of actual cases, have, through some fortuitous concourse of favourable circumstances, whether congenital or environmental, chanced to combine in producing an individual in whom many factors deviate from the norm in a socially advantageous manner.' Let us see if we can translate this sentence into English. I suggest the following: 'All men are scoundrels, or at any rate almost all. The men who are not must have had unusual luck, both in their birth and in their upbringing.' This is shorter and more intelligible, and says just the same thing. But I am afraid any professor who used the second sentence instead of the first would get the sack.

This suggests a word of advice to such of my readers as may happen to be professors. I am allowed to use plain English because everybody knows that I could use mathematical logic if I chose. Take the statement: 'Some people marry their deceased wives' sisters.' I can express this in language which only becomes intelligible after years of study, and this gives me freedom. I suggest to young professors that their first work should be written in a jargon only to be understood by the erudite few. With that behind them, they can ever after say what they have to say in a language 'understanded of the people.' In these days, when our very lives are at the mercy of the professors, I cannot but think that they would deserve our gratitude if they adopted my advice. (P. F. M., pages 213–214.)

Oppenheimer is disgraced and prevented from pursuing his work largely because he doubted the practicability of the hydrogen bomb at a time when this doubt was entirely rational. The F.B.I., which has only the level of education to be expected among policemen, considers itself competent to withhold visas from the most learned men in Europe on grounds which every person capable of understanding the matters at issue knows to be absurd. This evil has reached such a point that international conferences of learned men in the United States have become impossible. (P. F. M., page 137.)

Those who advocate common usage in philosophy sometimes speak in a manner that suggests the *mystique* of the 'common man.' They may admit that in organic chemistry there is need of long words, and that quantum physics requires formulas that are difficult to translate into ordinary English, but philosophy (they think) is different. It is not the function of philosophy —so they maintain—to teach something that uneducated people do not know; on the contrary, its function is to teach superior persons that they are not as superior as they thought they were, and that those who are *really* superior can show their skill by making sense of common sense.

No one wants to alter the language of common sense, any more than we wish to give up talking of the sun rising and setting. But astronomers find a different language better, and I contend that a different language is better in philosophy.

Let us take an example, that of perception. There is here an admixture of philosophical and scientific questions, but this admixture is inevitable in many questions, or, if not inevitable, can only be avoided by confining ourselves to comparatively unimportant aspects of the matter in hand.

Here is a series of questions and answers.

Q. When I see a table, will what I see be still there if I shut my eyes?

A. That depends upon the sense in which you use the word 'see.'

Q. What is still there when I shut my eyes?

A. This is an empirical question. Don't bother me with it, but ask the physicists.

Q. What exists when my eyes are open, but not when they are shut?

A. This again is empirical, but in deference to previous philosophers I will answer you: coloured surfaces.

Q. May I infer that there are two senses of 'see'? In the first, when I 'see' a table, I 'see' something conjectural about which physics has vague notions that are probably wrong. In the second, I 'see' coloured surfaces which cease to exist when I shut my eyes.

A. That is correct if you want to think clearly, but our philosophy makes clear thinking unnecessary. By oscillating between the two meanings, we avoid paradox and shock, which is more than most philosophers do. (P. F. M., pages 168, 170, 171, 172.)

V
POLITICS

ALTOGETHER LORD RUSSELL has had extensive experience with politics and with the effects of politics. His activities range from membership in the House of Lords to serving a term in prison for failing to agree with those in power on war policy.

During World War I he wrote a pamphlet in protest against the sentencing of a conscientious objector; for this he was fined one hundred pounds. A few months after this incident he was sentenced to six months' imprisonment for quoting the report of a congressional investigation into the use of federal troops against strikers. His pacifistic views crystallized when he said that neither the Allies nor the Central Powers could solve any problem by means of war. He changed his opinion, however, in the late thirties when Hitler and Mussolini made their totalitarian motives clear. During World War II he was a vigorous supporter of the free nations in the West. Since his visit to Russia in 1920 he has been a consistent opponent of Communism in both theory and practice.

With the advent of the atomic age a new question arose: Is victory possible for either side in an armed dispute? In the summer of 1955 he summoned news reporters from around the globe to listen to a last-minute appeal from a number of scientists regarding the possible effects of a war conducted with nuclear weapons. On July 9, 1955, just prior to the Summit meeting of the Big Four nations in Geneva, he met the Press to report the opinion of some of the most

eminent scientists of our time on this grave problem.
These scientists signed the following resolution: 'In
view of the fact that in any future world war nuclear
weapons will certainly be employed, and that such
weapons threaten the continued existence of mankind,
we urge the Governments of the world to realize, and
to acknowledge publicly, that their purposes cannot
be furthered by a world war, and we urge them,
consequently, to find peaceful means for the settlement
of all matters of dispute among them.' This resolution
was the outcome of a previous conference between
Lord Russell and Albert Einstein in which they decided a public appeal must be made to focus attention
on the problem of human survival in a modern war.
The resolution was written by Lord Russell and
signed by Einstein and nine other scientists. This was
Einstein's final word to humanity; he died the very
day Lord Russell received a letter from him confirm-
ing his agreement to this plea.

The kind of political structure Lord Russell would
wish to see is one in which power is apportioned with
more intelligence than it has been in the past. In his
opinion the central problem of political theory is 'how
to combine that degree of individual initiative which
is necessary for progress, with the degree of social
cohesion which is necessary for survival.' The history
of Western civilization has not been too encouraging
in this respect, but mankind now has at its disposal
weapons of universal extinction, which may cause
men to review their motives with grave concern.

Lord Russell has continued his efforts to persuade the
leaders of both East and West that a third World War
might, as he says, "put an end to the human race." At
eighty-six he is still one of the most active humanists in
our time.

The problems involved in international power politics in a scientific society are, without doubt, the most

serious men have had to face thus far. It is now imperative that men settle their political differences by some method other than war. Lord Russell's view is that society, such as we have at present, in which thought and technique are scientific, can be stable, given certain conditions. The minimum prerequisite conditions for peace are: a single government of the world with a monopoly of police power, a general diffusion of wealth so that no nation has special cause for envy, a low birth-rate throughout the world, and an atmosphere in which individual initiative in science, art, and play can thrive. Lord Russell freely admits that the world is a long way from achieving these noble objectives, but men can achieve them if they seriously choose to adopt them.

The wit that Lord Russell displays in the selections in this chapter is somewhat paradoxical. He is a very serious critic of politics and political theory but he is also one of the most trenchant satirists of this century. Most social critics fail to hold the interest of the reader because their style of writing is 'dry.' The reader who has gone this far will have discovered that Russell's style is anything but dull.

I am persuaded that there is absolutely no limit in the absurdities that can, by government action, come to be generally believed. Give me an adequate army, with power to provide it with more pay and better food than falls to the lot of the average man, and I will undertake, within thirty years, to make the majority of the population believe that two and two are three, that water freezes when it gets hot and boils when it gets cold, or any other nonsense that might seem to serve the interest of the State. Of course, even when these beliefs had been generated, people would not put the kettle in the refrigerator when they wanted it to boil. That cold makes water boil would be a Sunday truth, sacred and mystical, to be professed in awed tones, but not to be acted on in daily life. What would happen would be that any verbal denial of the mystic doctrine would be made illegal, and obstinate heretics would be 'frozen' at the stake. No person who did not enthusiastically accept the official doctrine would be allowed to teach or to have any position of power. Only the very highest officials, in their cups, would whisper to each other what rubbish it all is; then they would laugh and drink again. (U. E., pages 94–95.)

There are some desires which, though very powerful, have not, as a rule, any great *political* importance. Most men at some period of their lives desire to marry, but as a rule they can satisfy this desire without having to take any political action. There are, of course, exceptions; the rape of the Sabine women is a case in point. (N. P. A. S.)

When the British Government very unwisely allowed the Kaiser to be present at a naval review at Spithead, the thought which arose in his mind was not the one which we had intended. What he thought was: 'I must have a navy as good as Grandmama's.' And from this thought have sprung all our subsequent troubles. The world would be a happier place if acquisitiveness were always stronger than rivalry. But in fact, a great many men will cheerfully face impoverishment if they can thereby secure complete ruin for their rivals. Hence the present level of the income tax. (N. P. A. S.)

If politics is to become scientific, and if the event is not to be constantly surprising, it is imperative that our political thinking should penetrate more deeply into the springs of human action. What is the influence of hunger upon slogans? How does their effectiveness fluctuate with the number of calories in your diet? If one man offers you democracy and another offers you a bag of grain, at what stage of starvation will you prefer the grain to the vote? (N. P. A. S.)

One of the troubles about vanity is that it grows with what it feeds on. The more you are talked about, the more you will wish to be talked about. The con-demned murderer, I am told—I have had no personal experience—who is allowed to see the account of his trial in the Press is indignant if he finds a newspaper which has reported it inadequately. And the more he finds about himself in other newspapers, the more indignant he will be with the one whose reports are meagre. Politicians and literary men are in the same case. And the more famous they become, the more difficult the press cutting agency finds it to satisfy them. It is scarcely possible to exaggerate the influence of vanity throughout the range of human life, from the child of three to the potentate at whose frown the world trembles. Mankind have even committed the impiety of attributing similar desires to the Deity, whom they imagine avid for continual praise. (N. P. A. S.)

Most political leaders acquire their position by causing large numbers of people to believe that these leaders are actuated by altruistic desires. It is well understood that such a belief is more readily accepted under the influence of excitement. Brass bands, mob oratory, lynching, and war are stages in the development of the excitement. I suppose the advocates of unreason think that there is a better chance of profitably deceiving the populace if they keep it in a state of effervescence. Perhaps it is my dislike of this sort of process which leads people to say that I am unduly rational. (H. S. E. P., preface, page 10.)

The increase of organization has brought into existence new positions of power. Every body has to have executive officials, in whom, at any moment, its power is concentrated. It is true that officials are usually subject to control, but the control may be slow and distant. From the young lady who sells stamps in a post office all the way up to the Prime Minister, every official is invested, for the time being, with some part of the power of the State. You can complain of the young lady if her manners are bad, and you can vote against the Prime Minister at the next election if you disapprove of his policy. But both the young lady and the Prime Minister can have a very considerable run for their money before (if ever) your discontent has any effect. This increase in the power of officials is a constant source of irritation to everybody else. In most countries they are much less polite than in England; the police, especially in America for instance, seem to think you must be a rare exception if you are not a criminal. This tyranny of officials is one of the worst results of increasing organization, and one against which it is of the utmost importance to find safeguards if a scientific society is not to be intolerable to all but an insolent aristocracy of Jacks-in-office. (I. S. S., pages 48-9.)

Politics is largely governed by sententious platitudes which are devoid of truth. One of the most widespread popular maxims is, 'Human nature cannot be changed.' No one can say whether this is true or not without first defining 'human nature.' But as used it is certainly false. When Mr. A utters the maxim, with an air of portentous and conclusive wisdom, what he means is that all men everywhere will always continue to behave as they do in his own home town. A little anthropology will dispel this belief. Among the Tibetans, one wife has many husbands, because men are too poor to support a whole wife; yet family life, according to travellers, is no more unhappy than elsewhere. The practice of lending one's wife to a guest is very common among uncivilized tribes. The Australian aborigines, at puberty, undergo a very painful operation which, throughout the rest of their lives, greatly diminishes sexual potency. Infanticide, which might seem contrary to human nature, was almost universal before the rise of Christianity, and is recommended by Plato to prevent over-population. Private property is not recognized among some savage tribes. Even among highly civilized people, economic considerations will override what is called 'human nature.' (U. E., pages 121-2.)

The conscientious Radical is faced with great difficulties. He knows that he can increase his popularity by being false to his creed, and appealing to hatreds that have nothing to do with the reforms in which he believes. For example: a community that suffers from Japanese competition can easily be made indignant about bad labour conditions in Japan, and the unfair price-cutting that they render possible. But if the speaker goes on to say that it is Japanese *employers* who should be opposed, not Japanese *employees*, he will lose a large part of the sympathy of his audience. The Radical's only ultimate protection against demagogic appeals to misguided hatreds lies in education: he must convince intellectually a sufficient number of people to form the nucleus of a propagandist army. This is undoubtedly a difficult task, while the whole force of the State and the plutocracy is devoted to the fostering of unreason. But it is perhaps not so hopeless a task as many are now inclined to believe; and in any case it cannot be shirked, since the appeal to unreasoning emotion can always be better done by charlatans. (c. s., page 15, March 1936.)

I cannot be content with a brief moment of riotous living followed by destitution, and however clever the scientists may be, there are some things that they cannot be expected to achieve. When they have used up all the easily available sources of energy that nature has scattered carelessly over the surface of our planet, they will have to resort to more laborious processes, and these will involve a gradual lowering of the standard of living. Modern industrialists are like men who have come for the first time upon fertile virgin land, and can live for a little while in great comfort with only a modicum of labour. It would be irrational to hope that the present heyday of industrialism will not develop far beyond its present level, but sooner or later, owing to the exhaustion of raw material, its capacity to supply human needs will diminish, not suddenly, but gradually. This could, of course, be prevented if men exercised any restraint or foresight in their present frenzied exploitation. Perhaps before it is too late they will learn to do so. (N. H. C. W., page 37.)

How long will it be before the accessible oil in the world is exhausted? Will all the arable land be turned into dust-bowls as it has been in large parts of the United States? Will the population increase to the point where men again, like their remote ancestors, have no leisure to think of anything but the food supply? Such questions are not to be decided by general philosophical reflections. Communists think that there will be plenty of oil; if there are no capitalists. Some religious people think that there will be plenty of food if we trust in Providence. Such ideas are superficial, even when they are called scientific, as they are by the Communists. (N. H. C. W., pages 33–4.)

We all know that the price of food goes up, but most of us attribute this to the wickedness of the Government. If we live under a progressive Government, it makes us reactionary; if we live under a reactionary Government, it turns us into Socialists. Both these reactions are superficial and frivolous. All Governments, whatever their political complexion, are at present willy-nilly in the grip of natural forces which can only be dealt with by a degree of intelligence of which mankind hitherto has shown little evidence. (N. H. C. W., pages 38–9.)

I do not think any reasonable person can doubt that in India, China and Japan, if the knowledge of birth-control existed, the birth-rate would fall very rapidly. In Africa the process might take longer, but there also it could be fairly easily achieved if Negro doctors, trained in the West, were given the funds to establish medical clinics in which every kind of medical information would be given. I do not suppose that America would contribute to this beneficent work, because if either party favoured it, that party would lose the Catholic vote in New York State, and therefore the Presidency. This obviously would be a greater disaster than the extermination of the human race by atomic war. (N. H. C. W., page 144.)

Some opponents of Communism are attempting to produce an ideology for the Atlantic Powers, and for this purpose they have invented what they call 'Western Values.' These are supposed to consist of toleration, respect for individual liberty, and brotherly love. I am afraid this view is grossly unhistorical. If we compare Europe with other continents, it is marked out as the persecuting continent. Persecution only ceased after long and bitter experience of its futility; it continued as long as either Protestants or Catholics had any hope of exterminating the opposite party. The European record in this respect is far blacker than that of the Mohammedans, the Indians or the Chinese. No, if the West can claim superiority in anything, it is not in moral values but in science and scientific technique. (N. H. C. W., pages 118–119.)

Everything done by European administrators to improve the lot of Africans is, at present, totally and utterly futile because of the growth of population. The Africans, not unnaturally, though now mistakenly, attribute their destitution to their exploitation by the white man. If they achieve freedom suddenly before they have men trained in administration and a habit of responsibility, such civilization as white men have brought to Africa will quickly disappear. It is no use for doctrinaire liberals to deny this; there is a standing proof in the island of Haiti. (N. H. C. W., page 13.)

If two hitherto rival football teams, under the influence of brotherly love, decided to co-operate in placing the football first beyond one goal and then beyond the other, no one's happiness would be increased. There is no reason why the zest derived from competition should be confined to athletics. Emulation between teams or localities or organizations can be a useful incentive. But if competition is not to become ruthless and harmful, the penalty for failure must not be disaster, as in war, or starvation, as in unregulated economic competition, but only loss of glory. Football would not be a desirable sport if defeated teams were put to death or left to starve. (A. I., page 72.)

In a shipwreck the crew obey orders without the need of reasoning with themselves, because they have a common purpose which is not remote, and the means to its realization are not difficult to understand. But if the Captain were obliged, like the Government, to explain the principles of currency in order to prove his commands wise, the ship would sink before his lecture was finished. (A. I., page 68.)

The savage, in spite of his membership of a small community, lived a life in which his initiative was not too much hampered by the community. The things that he wanted to do, usually hunting and war, were also the things that his neighbours wanted to do, and if he felt an inclination to become a medicine man he only had to ingratiate himself with some individual already eminent in that profession, and so, in due course, to succeed to his powers of magic. If he was a man of exceptional talent, he might invent some improvement in weapons, or a new skill in hunting. These would not put him into any opposition to the community, but, on the contrary, would be welcomed. The modern man lives a very different life. If he sings in the street he will be thought to be drunk and if he dances a policeman will reprove him for impeding the traffic. (A. I., page 60.)

Two great religions—Buddhism and Christianity—have sought to extend to the whole human race the co-operative feeling that is spontaneous towards fellow tribesmen. They have preached the brotherhood of man, showing by the use of the word 'brotherhood' that they are attempting to extend beyond its natural bounds an emotional attitude which, in its origin, is biological. If we are all children of God, then we are all one family. But in practice those who in theory adopted this creed have always felt that those who did not adopt it were not children of God but children of Satan, and the old mechanism of hatred of those outside the tribe has returned, giving added vigour to the creed, but in a direction which diverted it from its original purpose. Religion, morality, economic self-interest, the mere pursuit of biological survival, all supply to our intelligence unanswerable arguments in favour of world-wide co-operation, but the old instincts that have come down to us from our tribal ancestors rise up in indignation, feeling that life would lose its savour if there were no one to hate, that anyone who could love such a scoundrel as So-and-so would be a worm, that struggle is the law of life, and that in a world where we all loved one another there would be nothing to live for. (A. I., pages 19–20.)

Before the war (World War I) one of the objections commonly urged against votes for women was that women would tend to be pacifists. During the war they gave a large-scale refutation of this charge, and the vote was given to them for their share in the bloody work. (M. M., page 67.)

There are many points of view from which the life of man may be considered. There are those who think of him primarily in cultural terms as being capable of lofty art and sublime speculation and discovery of the hidden secrets of nature. There are those who think of him as one of those kinds of animals that are capable of government, though in this respect he is completely outshone by ants and bees. There are those who think of him as the master of war; these include all the men in all countries who decide upon the adornment of public squares, where it is an invariable rule obeyed by all right-thinking public authorities that the most delectable object to be seen by the passers-by is a man on horseback, who is commemorated for his skill in homicide. (N. H. C. W., page 41.)

Organizations are of two kinds, those which aim at getting something done, and those which aim at preventing something from being done. The Post Office is an example of the first kind; a fire brigade is an example of the second kind. Neither of these arouses much controversy, because no one objects to letters being carried, and incendiaries dare not avow a desire to see buildings burnt down. But when what is to be prevented is something done by human beings, not by Nature, the matter is otherwise. The armed forces of one's own nation exist—so each nation asserts—to PREVENT aggression by other nations. But the armed forces of other nations exist—or so many people believe—to PROMOTE aggression. If you say anything against the armed forces of your own country, you are a traitor, wishing to see your fatherland ground under the heel of a brutal conqueror. If, on the other hand, you defend a potential enemy State for thinking armed forces necessary to its safety, you malign your own country, whose unalterable devotion to peace only perverse malice could lead you to question. I heard all this said about Germany by a thoroughly virtuous German lady in 1936, in the course of a panegyric on Hitler. (I. s. s., pages 54–5.)

I do not pretend that birth control is the only way in which population can be kept from increasing. There are others, which, one must suppose, opponents of birth control would prefer. War . . . has hitherto been disappointing in this respect, but perhaps bacteriological war may prove more effective. If a Black Death could be spread throughout the world once in every generation survivors could procreate freely without making the world too full. There would be nothing in this to offend the consciences of the devout or to restrain the ambitions of nationalists. The state of affairs might be somewhat unpleasant, but what of that? Really high-minded people are indifferent to happiness, especially other people's. (I. s. s., pages 127–8.)

In superstitious moments I am tempted to believe in the myth of the Tower of Babel, and to suppose that in our own day a similar but greater impiety is about to be visited by a more tragic and terrible punishment.

Perhaps—so I sometimes allow myself to fancy—God does not intend us to understand the mechanism by which He regulates the material universe. Perhaps the nuclear physicists have come so near to the ultimate secrets that He thinks it time to bring their activities to a stop. And what simpler method could He devise than to let them carry their ingenuity to the point where they exterminate the human race? If I could think that deer and squirrels, nightingales and larks, would survive, I might view this catastrophe with some equanimity, since man has not shown himself worthy to be the lord of creation. But it is to be feared that the dreadful alchemy of the atomic bomb will destroy all forms of life equally, and that the earth will remain forever a dead clod senselessly whirling round a futile sun. I do not know the immediate precipitating cause of this interesting occurrence. Perhaps it will be a dispute about Persian oil, perhaps a disagreement as to Chinese trade, perhaps a quarrel between Jews and Mohammedans for the control of Palestine. Any patriotic person can see that these issues are of such importance as to make the extermination of mankind preferable to cowardly conciliation. (U. E., pages 173–4.)

Men, quite ordinary men, will compel children to look on while their mothers are raped. In pursuit of political aims men will submit their opponents to long years of unspeakable anguish. We know what the Nazis did to Jews at Auschwitz. In mass cruelty, the expulsions of Germans ordered by the Russians fall not very far short of the atrocities perpetrated by the Nazis. And how about our noble selves? We would not do such deeds. Oh no! But we enjoy our juicy steaks and our hot rolls while German children die of hunger because our governments dare not face our indignation if they asked us to forgo some part of our pleasures. If there were a Last Judgment as Christians believe, how do you think our excuses would sound before that final tribunal? (U. E., page 175.)

Stalin could neither understand nor respect the point of view which led Churchill to allow himself to be peaceably dispossessed as a result of a popular vote. I am a firm believer in democratic representative government as the best form for those who have the tolerance and self-restraint that is required to make it workable. But its advocates make a mistake if they suppose that it can be at once introduced into countries where the average citizen has hitherto lacked all training in the give-and-take that it requires. In a Balkan country, not so many years ago, a party which had been beaten by a narrow margin in a general election retrieved its fortunes by shooting a sufficient number of the representatives of the other side to give it a majority. People in the West thought this characteristic of the Balkans, forgetting that Cromwell and Robespierre had acted likewise. (U. E., pages 180–1.)

The American legislators who made the immigration laws consider the Nordics superior to Slavs or Latins or any other white men. But the Nazis, under the stress of war, were led to the conclusion that there are hardly any true Nordics outside Germany; the Norwegians, except Quisling and his few followers, had been corrupted by intermixture with Finns and Lapps and such. Thus politics are a clue to descent. The biologically pure Nordics love Hitler, and if you did not love Hitler, that was proof of tainted blood. (U. E., page 117.)

Very little remains of institutions and ways of life that when I was a child appeared as indestructible as granite. I grew up in an atmosphere impregnated with tradition. My parents died before I can remember, and I was brought up by my grandparents. . . . I was taught a kind of theoretic republicanism which was prepared to tolerate a monarch so long as he recognized that he was an employee of the people and subject to dismissal if he proved unsatisfactory. My grandfather, who was no respecter of persons, used to explain this point of view to Queen Victoria, and she was not altogether sympathetic. She did, however, give him the house in Richmond Park in which I spent all my youth. I imbibed certain political principles and expectations, and have on the whole retained the former in spite of being compelled to reject the latter. There was to be ordered progress throughout the world, no revolutions, a gradual cessation of war, and an extension of parliamentary government to all those unfortunate regions which did not yet enjoy it. My grandmother used to laugh about a conversation she had had with the Russian Ambassador. She said to him, 'Perhaps some day you will have a parliament in Russia,' and he replied, 'God forbid, my dear Lady John.' The Russian Ambassador of today might give the same answer if he changed the first word. (P. F. M., pages 7, 8.)

Neither misery nor folly seems to me any part of the inevitable lot of man. And I am convinced that intelligence, patience, and eloquence can, sooner or later, lead the human race out of its self-imposed tortures provided it does not exterminate itself meanwhile.

On the basis of this belief, I have had always a certain degree of optimism, although, as I have grown older, the optimism has grown more sober and the happy issue more distant. But I remain completely incapable of agreeing with those who accept fatalistically the view that man is born to trouble. The causes of unhappiness in the past and in the present are not difficult to ascertain. There have been poverty, pestilence, and famine, which were due to man's inadequate mastery of nature. There have been wars, oppressions and tortures which have been due to men's hostility to their fellow men. And there have been morbid miseries fostered by gloomy creeds, which have led men into profound inner discords that made all outward prosperity of no avail. All these are unnecessary. In regard to all of them, means are known by which they can be overcome. In the modern world, if communities are unhappy, it is because they choose to be so. Or to speak more precisely, because they have ignorances, habits, beliefs, and passions, which are dearer to them than happiness or even life. I find many men in our dangerous age who seem to be in love with misery and death, and who grow angry when hopes are suggested to them. (P. F. M., pages 53–4.)

VI

ETHICS

THE KIND OF ETHIC that Lord Russell proposes is one devoid of fear, superstition, and organized madness, where emotions are strong—but not destructive—and where men love each other as vehemently as they now desire the misery of their enemies. Though it would seem that sane men everywhere would agree with this proposal as a basis for ethics, mankind as a whole has not been influenced to any appreciable degree towards a realization of these objectives.

As the selections in this chapter will reveal, Lord Russell shaves the dogma from a number of superstitious beliefs and each, in turn, is left naked with nowhere to hide. Consider, for example, the question of voluntary euthanasia. Are civilized men really expected to believe that 'A wise, omnipotent and beneficent Being finds so much pleasure in watching the slow agonies of an innocent person that He will be angry with those who shorten the ordeal?' It is this sort of sardonic criticism of traditional beliefs that gives these selections that unmistakable Russell touch. Clarity, wit and fluency of expression have made his writings a joy to the layman.

In ethics, as elsewhere, Lord Russell has been accused of being unduly 'rational.' At any rate, it has been said by a number of his critics that his ethic is based upon reason alone. This opinion is wholly false. Reason has nothing to do with the selection of noble or heinous ends. It is only a regulator, and as such, reason is merely the selection of the appropriate means to an objective you wish to attain. The ends of any ethic cannot be proved by reason; all we can say is that we desire certain ends and not others. You may wish to promote the general happiness of mankind while your neighbour may wish to retain this only for his friends and keep his enemies in perpetual slavery. In neither case are we *logically* compelled to agree.

The kind of world Lord Russell would wish to see is one devoid of harmful myths, and where men are dedicated to the tasks of acquiring knowledge and skill not to kill each other, but to increase happiness. Such a world would include helpful emotions—sympathy, love, and genuine kindliness—and sufficient harmless outlets for individual initiative in both work and play.

Measures of sterilization should, in my opinion, be very definitely confined to persons who are *mentally* defective. I cannot favour laws such as that of Idaho, which allows sterilization of 'mental defectives, epileptics, habitual criminals, moral degenerates, and sex perverts.' The last two categories here are very vague, and will be determined differently in different communities. The law of Idaho would have justified the sterilization of Socrates, Plato, Julius Caesar, and St. Paul. (M. M., pages 259, 260.)

In addition to the general argument against faith, there is something peculiarly odious in the contention that the principles of the Sermon on the Mount are to be adopted with a view to making atom bombs more effective. If I were a Christian, I should consider this the absolute extreme of blasphemy. (H. S. E. P., page 221.)

If throughout your life you abstain from murder, theft, fornication, perjury, blasphemy, and disrespect towards your parents, your Church, and your king, you are conventionally held to deserve moral admiration even if you have never done a single kind or generous or useful action. This very inadequate notion of virtue is an outcome of tabu morality, and has done untold harm. (H. S. E. P., page 40.)

The Russian Government appears to think that Soviet decrees can change the laws of genetics; the Vatican apparently believes that ecclesiastical decrees could secure adequate nourishment for us all, even if there were only standing room on the planet. Such opinions, to my mind, represent a form of insane megalomania entirely alien to the scientific spirit. (N. H. C. W., page 27.)

Christ said 'Thou shalt love thy neighbour as thyself,' and when asked 'who is thy neighbour?' went on to the parable of the Good Samaritan. If you wish to understand this parable as it was understood by His hearers, you should substitute 'German' or 'Japanese' for 'Samaritan.' I fear many present-day Christians would resent such a substitution, because it would compel them to realize how far they have departed from the teaching of the Founder of their religion. (U. E., page 136.)

Suppose atomic bombs had reduced the population of the world to one brother and sister; should they let the human race die out? I do not know the answer, but I do not think it can be in the affirmative merely on the ground that incest is wicked. (H. S. E. P., page 47.)

The whole conception of 'sin' is one I find very puzzling, doubtless owing to my sinful nature. If 'sin' consisted in causing needless suffering, I could understand, but on the contrary, sin often consists in avoiding needless suffering. Some years ago, in the English House of Lords, a bill was introduced to legalize euthanasia in cases of painful and incurable disease. The patient's consent was to be necessary, as well as several medical certificates. To me, in my simplicity, it would seem natural to require the patient's consent, but the late Archbishop of Canterbury, the English official expert on sin, explained the erroneousness of such a view. The patient's consent turns euthanasia into suicide, and suicide is sin. Their Lordships listened to the voice of authority and rejected the bill. Consequently, to please the Archbishop—and his God, if he reports truly—victims of cancer still have to endure months of wholly useless agony, unless their doctors or nurses are sufficiently humane to risk a charge of murder. I find difficulty in the conception of a God who gets pleasure from contemplating such tortures; and if there were a God capable of such wanton cruelty, I should certainly not think Him worthy of worship. But that only proves how sunk I am in moral depravity. (U. E., page 76.)

Has civilization taught us to be more friendly towards one another? The answer is easy. Robins (the English, not the American species) peck an elderly robin to death, whereas men (the English, not the American species) give an elderly man an old-age pension. Within the herd we are more friendly to each other than are many species of animals, but in our attitude towards those outside the herd, in spite of all that has been done by moralists and religious teachers, our emotions are as ferocious as those of any animal, and our intelligence enables us to give them a scope which is denied to even the most savage beast. It may be hoped, though not very confidently, that the more humane attitude will in time come to prevail, but so far the omens are not very propitious. (U. E., page 126.)

There is in Aristotle an almost complete absence of what may be called benevolence or philanthropy. The sufferings of mankind, in so far as he is aware of them, do not move him emotionally; he holds them intellectually to be an evil, but there is no evidence that they cause him unhappiness except when the sufferers happen to be his friends. (H. W. P., pages 183, 184.)

Most stern moralists are in the habit of thinking of pleasure as only of the senses, and, when they eschew the pleasures of sense, they do not notice that the pleasures of power, which to men of their temperament are far more attractive, have not been brought within the ban of their ascetic self-denial. It is the prevalence of this type of psychology in forceful men which has made the notion of sin so popular, since it combines so perfectly humility towards heaven with self-assertion here on earth. The concept of sin has not the hold upon men's imaginations that it had in the Middle Ages, but still dominates the thoughts of many clergymen, magistrates and schoolmasters. When the great Dr. Arnold walked on the shores of Lake Como, it was not the beauty of the scene that occupied his thoughts. He meditated, so he tells us, on moral evil. I rather fear that it was the moral evil of school-boys rather than school-masters that produced his melancholy reflections. However that may be, he was led to the unshakable belief that it is good for boys to be flogged. One of the great rewards that a belief in sin has always offered to the virtuous is the opportunity which it affords of inflicting pain without compunction. (H. S. E. P., pages 195–6.)

One of the 'grand' conceptions which have proved scientifically useless is the soul. I do not mean that there is positive evidence showing that men have no soul; I only mean that the soul, if it exists, plays no part in any discoverable causal law. There are all kinds of experimental methods of determining how men and animals behave under various circumstances. You can put rats in mazes and men in barbed-wire cages, and observe their methods of escape. You can administer drugs and observe their effect. You can turn a male rat into a female, though so far nothing analogous has been done with human beings, even at Buchenwald. It appears that socially undesirable conduct can be dealt with by medical means, or by creating a better environment, and the conception of sin has thus come to seem quite unscientific, except, of course, as applied to the Nazis. There is real hope that, by getting to understand the science of human behaviour, governments may be even more able than they are at present to turn mankind into rabbles of mutually ferocious lunatics. (U. E., pages 133, 134.)

Cotton goods (after the industry became scientific) could find a market in India and Africa: this was a stimulus to British Imperialism. Africans had to be taught that nudity is wicked; this was done very cheaply by missionaries. In addition to cotton goods we exported tuberculosis and syphilis, but for them there was no charge. (I. S. S., page 21.)

As soon as we abandon our own reason, and are content to rely upon authority, there is no end to our trouble. Whose authority? The Old Testament? The New Testament? The Koran? In practice, people choose the book considered sacred by the community in which they are born, and out of that book they choose the parts they like, ignoring the others. At one time, the most influential text in the Bible was: 'Thou shalt not suffer a witch to live.' Nowadays, people pass over this text, in silence if possible; if not, with an apology. And so, even when we have a sacred book, we still choose as truth whatever suits our own prejudices. No Catholic, for instance, takes seriously the text which says that a Bishop should be the husband of one wife. (U. E., pages 81–82.)

Consider how much brutality has been justified by the rhyme:

> A dog, a wife, and a walnut tree,
> The more you beat them the better they be.

I have no experience of the moral effect of flagellation on walnut trees, but no civilized person would now justify the rhyme as regards wives. The reformative effect of punishment is a belief that dies hard, chiefly, I think, because it is so satisfying to our sadistic impulses. (U. E., page 148.)

I had at one time a very bad fever of which I almost died. In my fever I had a long consistent delirium. I dreamt that I was in Hell, and that Hell is a place full of all those happenings that are improbable but not impossible. The effects of this are curious. Some of the damned, when they first arrive below, imagine that they will beguile the tedium of eternity by games of cards. But they find this impossible, because, whenever a pack is shuffled, it comes out in perfect order, beginning with the ace of spades and ending with the king of hearts. There is a special department of Hell for students of probability. In this department there are many typewriters and many monkeys. Every time that a monkey walks on a typewriter, it types by chance one of Shakespeare's sonnets. . . .

There is a peculiarly painful chamber inhabited solely by philosophers who have refuted Hume. These philosophers, though in Hell, have not learned wisdom. They continue to be governed by their animal propensity toward induction. But every time that they have made an induction, the next instance falsifies it. This, however, happens only during the first hundred years of their damnation. After that, they learn to expect that an induction will be falsified, and therefore it is not falsified until another century of logical torment has altered their expectation. Throughout all eternity surprise continues, but each time at a higher logical level. (N. E. P., pages 30, 31.)

When we pass in review the opinions of former times which are now recognized as absurd, it will be found that nine times out of ten they were such as to justify the infliction of suffering. Take, for instance, medical practice. When anaesthetics were invented they were thought to be wicked as being an attempt to thwart God's will. Insanity was thought to be due to diabolic possession, and it was believed that demons inhabiting a madman could be driven out by inflicting pain upon him, and so making them uncomfortable. In pursuit of this opinion, lunatics were treated for years on end with systematic and conscientious brutality. I cannot think of any instance of an erroneous medical treatment that was agreeable rather than disagreeable to the patient. (U. E., page 148.)

The absence of any sharp line between men and apes is very awkward for theology. When did men get souls? Was the Missing Link capable of sin and therefore worthy of hell? Did Pithecanthropus Erectus have moral responsibility? Was Homo Pekiniensis damned? (I. S. S., pages 15, 16.)

A man who uses what is called 'bad language' is not from a rational point of view any worse than a man who does not. Nevertheless practically everybody in trying to imagine a saint would consider abstinence from swearing as essential. Considered in the light of reason this is simply silly. The same applies to alcohol and tobacco. With regard to alcohol the feeling does not exist in southern countries, and indeed there is an element of impiety about it, since it is known that Our Lord and the Apostles drank wine. With regard to tobacco it is easier to maintain a negative position, since all the greatest saints lived before its use was known. But here also no rational argument is possible. The view that no saint would smoke is based in the last analysis upon the view that no saint would do anything solely because it gave him pleasure. (C. H., page 99.)

When Benjamin Franklin invented the lightning-rod, the clergy, both in England and America, with enthusiastic support of George III, condemned it as an impious attempt to defeat the will of God. For, as all right-thinking people were aware, lightning is sent by God to punish impiety or some other grave sin— the virtuous are never struck by lightning. Therefore if God wants to strike anyone, Benjamin Franklin ought not to defeat His design; indeed, to do so is helping criminals to escape. But God was equal to the occasion, if we are to believe the eminent Dr. Price, one of the leading divines of Boston. Lightning having been rendered ineffectual by the 'iron points invented by the sagacious Dr. Franklin,' Massachusetts was shaken by earthquakes, which Dr. Price perceived to be due to God's wrath at the 'iron points.' In a sermon on the subject he said, 'In Boston are more erected than elsewhere in New England, and Boston seems to be more dreadfully shaken. Oh! There is no getting out of the mighty hand of God.' Apparently, however, Providence gave up all hope of curing Boston of its wickedness, for, though the lightning-rods became more and more common, earthquakes in Massachusetts have remained rare. Nevertheless, Dr. Price's point of view, or something very like it, was still held by one of the most influential men of recent times. When, at one time, there were several bad earthquakes in India, Mahatma Gandhi solemnly warned his compatriots that these disasters had been sent as a punishment for their sins. (U. E., pages 74–75.)

There are logical difficulties in the notion of Sin. We are told that Sin consists in acting contrary to God's commands, but we are also told that God is omnipotent. If He is, nothing contrary to His will can occur; therefore when the sinner disobeys His commands, He must have intended this to happen. St. Augustine boldly accepts this view, and asserts that men are led to sin by a blindness with which God afflicts them. But most theologians, in modern times, have felt that, if God causes men to sin, it is not fair to send them to Hell for what they cannot help. We are told that sin consists in acting contrary to God's will. This, however, does not get rid of the difficulty. Those who, like Spinoza, take God's omnipotence seriously, deduce that there can be no such thing as Sin. This leads to frightful results. What! said Spinoza's contemporaries, was it not wicked of Nero to murder his mother? Was it not wicked of Adam to eat the apple? Is one action just as good as another? Spinoza wriggles, but does not find any satisfactory answer. *If* everything happens in accordance with God's will, God must have wanted Nero to murder his mother; therefore, since God is good, the murder must have been a good thing. From this argument there is no escape. (U. E., pages 80–81.)

The Roman Catholic Church demands legislation such that, if a woman becomes pregnant by a syphilitic man, she must not artificially interrupt her pregnancy, but must allow a probably syphilitic child to be born, in order that, after a few years of misery on earth, it may spend eternity in limbo (assuming its parents to be non-Catholics). The British State considers it the duty of an Englishman to kill people who are not English whenever a collection of elderly gentlemen in Westminster tells him to do so. Such instances suffice to illustrate the fact that Church and State are im-

placable enemies of both intelligence and virtue. (E.
s. o., page 72.)

Suppose we wish—as I certainly do—to find arguments
against Nietzsche's ethics and politics, what arguments
can we find? . . . The question is: If Buddha and
Nietzsche were confronted, could either produce an
argument that ought to appeal to the impartial listener?
I am not thinking of political arguments. We can
imagine them appearing before the Almighty, as in
the first chapter of the Book of Job, and offering advice as to the sort of world He should create. What
could either say?

Buddha would open the argument by speaking of
the lepers, outcast and miserable; the poor, toiling with
aching limbs and barely kept alive by scanty nourishment; the wounded in battle, dying in slow agony;
the orphans, ill-treated by cruel guardians; and even
the most successful haunted by the thought of failure
and death. From all this load of sorrow, he would say,
a way of salvation must be found, and salvation can
only come through love.

Nietzsche, whom only Omnipotence could restrain
from interrupting, would burst out when his turn
came: 'Good heavens, man, you must learn to be of
tougher fibre. Why go about snivelling because trivial
people suffer. Or, for that matter, because great men
suffer? Trivial people suffer trivially, great men suffer
greatly, they are noble. Your ideal is a purely negative one, absence of suffering, which can be completely
secured by non-existence. I, on the other hand, have
positive ideals: I admire Alcibiades, and the Emperor
Frederick II, and Napoleon. For the sake of such men,
any misery is worth while. I appeal to You, Lord, as
the greatest of creative artists, do not let Your artistic
impulses be curbed by the degenerate, fear-ridden
maunderings of this wretched psychopath.'

Buddha, who in the courts of Heaven has learnt all history since his death, and has mastered science with delight in the knowledge and sorrow at the use to which men have put it, replies with calm urbanity: 'You are mistaken, Professor Nietzsche, in thinking my ideal a purely negative one. True, it includes a negative element, the absence of suffering; but it has in addition quite as much that is positive as is to be found in your doctrine. Though I have no special admiration for Alcibiades and Napoleon, I too have my heroes: My successor Jesus, because he told men to love their enemies; the men who discovered how to master the forces of nature and secure food with less labour; the medical men who have shown how to diminish disease; the poets and artists and musicians who have caught glimpses of the Divine beatitude. Love and knowledge and delight in beauty are not negations; they are enough to fill the lives of the great men that have ever lived.'

'All the same,' Nietzsche replies, 'your world would be insipid. You should study Heraclitus, whose works survive complete in the celestial library. Your love is compassion, which is elicited by pain; your truth, if you are honest, is pleasant, and only to be known through suffering; and as to beauty, what is more beautiful than the tiger, who owes his splendour to fierceness? No, if the Lord should decide for your world, I fear we should all die of boredom.'

'You might,' Buddha replies, 'because you love pain, and your love of life is a sham. But those who really love life would be happy as no one can be happy in the world as it is.' (H. W. P., pages 770, 771, 772.)

According to St. Thomas, evil is unintentional, not as essence, and has an accidental cause which is good. All things tend to be like God, who is the End of all things. Human happiness does not consist in carnal pleasures, honour, glory, wealth, worldly power, or goods of the body, and is not seated in the sense. Man's ultimate happiness does not consist in acts of moral virtue, because these are means; it consists in the contemplation of God. But the knowledge of God possessed by the majority does not suffice; nor the knowledge of Him obtained by faith. In this life, we cannot see God in His essence, or have ultimate happiness; but hereafter we shall see Him face to face. (Not literally, we are warned, because God has no face.) This will happen not by our natural power, but by the divine light; and even then, we shall not see all of Him. (H. W. P., pages 458–459.)

Those who first advocated religious toleration were thought wicked, and so were the early opponents of slavery. The Gospels tell how Christ opposed the stricter forms of the Sabbath tabu. It cannot, in view of such instances, be denied that some actions which we all think highly laudable consist in criticizing or infringing the moral code of one's own community. Of course this only applies to past ages or to foreigners; nothing of the sort could occur among ourselves, since our moral code is perfect. (H. S. E. P., pages 39 and 40.)

Protestants tell us, or used to tell us, that it is contrary to the will of God to work on Sundays. But Jews say that it is on Saturdays that God objects to work. Disagreement on this point has persisted for nineteen centuries, and I know no method of putting an end to the disagreement except Hitler's lethal chambers, which would not generally be regarded as a legitimate method in scientific controversy. Jews and Mohammedans assure us that God forbids pork, but Hindus say that it is beef that he forbids. Disagreement on this point has caused hundreds of thousands to be massacred in recent years. It can hardly be said, therefore,

that the Will of God gives a basis for an objective
ethic. (H. S. E. P., page 121.)

I know men, by no means old, who, when in infancy
they were seen touching a certain portion of their
body, were told with the utmost solemnity: 'I would
rather see you dead than doing that.' I regret to say
that the effect in producing virtue in later life has not
always been all that conventional moralists might desire. Not infrequently threats are used. It is perhaps
not so common as it used to be to threaten a child with
castration, but it is still thought quite proper to
threaten him with insanity. Indeed, it is illegal in the
State of New York to let him know that he does not
run the risk unless he thinks he does. The result of this
teaching is that most children in their earliest years
have a profound sense of guilt and terror which is associated with sexual matters. This association of sex with
guilt and fear goes so deep as to become almost or
wholly unconscious. I wish it were possible to insti-
tute a statistical inquiry, among men who believe
themselves emancipated from such nursery tales, as to
whether they would be as ready to commit adultery
during a thunderstorm as at any other time. I believe
that 90 per cent of them, in their heart of hearts,
would think that if they did so they would be struck
by lightning. (M. M., pages 275–276.)

The Platonic Socrates was a pattern to subsequent
philosophers for many ages. What are we to think of
him ethically? (I am concerned only with the man as
Plato portrays him.) His merits are obvious. He is indifferent to worldly success, so devoid of fear that he
remains calm and urbane and humorous to the last moment, caring more for what he believes to be truth
than for anything else whatever. He has, however,
some grave defects. He is dishonest and sophistical in

argument, and in his private thinking he uses intellect to prove conclusions that are to him agreeable, rather than in a disinterested search for knowledge. There is something smug and unctuous about him, which reminds one of a bad type of cleric. His courage in the face of death would have been more remarkable if he had not believed that he was going to enjoy eternal bliss in the company of the gods. Unlike some of his predecessors, he was not scientific in his thinking, but was determined to prove the universe agreeable to his ethical standards. This is treachery to truth, and the worst of philosophic sins. As a man, we may believe him admitted to the communion of saints; but as a philosopher he needs a long residence in a scientific purgatory. (H. W. P., pages 142–143.)

Since reason consists in a just adaptation of means to ends, it can only be opposed by those who think it a good thing that people should choose means which cannot realize their professed ends. This implies either that they should be deceived as to how to realize their professed ends, or that their real ends should not be those that they profess. The first is the case of a populace misled by an eloquent *fuehrer*. The second is that of the schoolmaster who enjoys torturing boys, but wishes to go on thinking himself a benevolent humanitarian. I cannot feel that either of these grounds for opposing reason is morally respectable. (H. S. E. P., preface, page 10.)

One critic takes me to task because I say that only evil passions prevent the realization of a better world, and goes on triumphantly to ask, 'are all human emotions necessarily evil?' In the very book that leads my critic to this objection, I say that what the world needs is Christian love, or compassion. This, surely, is an emotion, and, in saying that this is what the world needs, I am not suggesting reason as a driving force. I can only suppose that this emotion, because it is neither cruel nor destructive, is not attractive to the apostles of unreason. (H. S. E. P., preface, page 9.)

Intellectually, the effect of mistaken moral considerations upon philosophy has been to impede progress to an extraordinary extent. I do not myself believe that philosophy can either prove or disprove the truth of religious dogmas, but ever since Plato most philosophers have considered it part of their business to produce 'proofs' of immortality and the existence of God. They have found fault with the proofs of their predecessors—St. Thomas rejected St. Anselm's proofs, and Kant rejected Descartes'—but they have supplied new ones of their own. In order to make their proofs seem valid, they have had to falsify logic, to make mathematics mystical, and to pretend that deep-seated prejudices were heaven-sent intuitions. (H. W. P., page 835.)

All who are not lunatics are agreed about certain things: That it is better to be alive than dead, better to be adequately fed than starved, better to be free than a slave. Many people desire those things only for themselves and their friends; they are quite content that their enemies should suffer. These people can be refuted by science: Mankind has become so much one family that we cannot insure our own prosperity except by insuring that of everyone else. If you wish to be happy yourself, you must resign yourself to seeing others also happy. (S. S. S., page 33.)

The Stoic-Christian view requires a conception of virtue very different from Aristotle's, since it must hold that virtue is as possible for the slave as for his master. Christian ethics disapproves of pride, which Aristotle thinks a virtue, and praises humility, which he thinks a vice. The intellectual virtues, which Plato and Aristotle value above all others, have to be thrust out of the list altogether, in order that the poor and humble may be able to be as virtuous as anyone else. Pope Gregory the Great solemnly reproved a bishop for teaching grammar. (H. W. P., page 177.)

There is no pretence of justice, as we understand it, in the punishment following an act forbidden by a tabu, which is rather to be conceived as analogous to death as the result of touching a live wire. When David was transporting the Ark on a cart, it jolted over a rough threshing floor, and Uzzah, who was in charge, thinking it would fall, stretched up his hand to steady it. For this impiety, in spite of his laudable motive, he was struck dead (II Samuel vi. 6–7). The same lack of justice appears in the fact that not only murder, but accidental homicide, calls for purification. (H. S. E. P., page 29.)

It must be admitted that there is a certain type of Christian ethic to which Nietzsche's strictures can be justly applied. Pascal and Dostoevsky—his own illustrations—have both something abject in their virtue. Pascal sacrificed his magnificent mathematical intellect to his God, thereby attributing to Him a barbarity which was a cosmic enlargement of Pascal's morbid mental tortures. Dostoevsky would have nothing to do with 'proper pride'; he would sin in order to repent and to enjoy the luxury of confession. (H. W. P., page 768.)

Forms of morality based on tabu linger on into civilized communities to a greater extent than some people realize. Pythagoras forbade beans, and Empedocles thought it wicked to munch laurel leaves. Hindus shudder at the thought of eating beef; Mohammedans and orthodox Jews regard the flesh of the pig as unclean. St. Augustine, the missionary to Britain, wrote to Pope Gregory the Great to know whether married people might come to church if they had had intercourse the previous night, and the Pope ruled that they might only do so after a ceremonial washing. There was a law in Connecticut—I believe it is still formally unrepealed—making it illegal for a man to kiss his wife on Sunday. (H. S. E. P., pages 29–30.)

It is true that if we ever did stop to think about the cosmos we might find it uncomfortable. The sun may grow cold or blow up; the earth may lose its atmosphere and become uninhabitable. Life is a brief, small, and transitory phenomenon in an obscure corner, not at all the sort of thing that one would make a fuss about if one were not personally concerned. But it is monkish and futile—so scientific man will say—to dwell on such cold and unpractical thoughts. Let us get on with the job of fertilizing the desert, melting Arctic ice, and killing each other with perpetually improving technique. Some of our activities will do good, some harm, but all alike will show our power. And so, in this godless universe, we shall become gods. (I. S. S., page 15.)

Law in origin was merely a codification of the power of dominant groups, and did not aim at anything that to a modern man would appear to be justice. In many Germanic tribes, for example, if you committed a murder, you were fined, and the fine depended upon the social status of your victim. Wherever aristocracy existed, its members had various privileges which were not accorded to the plebs. In Japan before the Meiji era began a man who omitted to smile in the presence of a social superior could legally be killed then and

there by the superior in question. This explains why
European travellers find the Japanese a smiling race.
(N. H. C. W., page 75.)

The Christian ethics inevitably, through the emphasis
laid upon sexual virtue, did a great deal to degrade the
position of women. Since the moralists were men,
woman appeared as the temptress; if they had been
women, man would have had this role. Since woman
was the temptress, it was desirable to curtail her opportunities for leading men into temptation; consequently respectable women were more and more
hedged about with restrictions, while the women who
were not respectable, being regarded as sinful, were
treated with the utmost contumely. It is only in quite
modern times that women have regained the degree of
freedom which they enjoyed in the Roman Empire.
The patriarchal system . . . did much to enslave
women, but a great deal of this was undone just before
the rise of Christianity. After Constantine, women's
freedom was again curtailed under the pretence of
protecting them from sin. It is only with the decay of
the notion of sin in modern times that women have
begun to regain their freedom. (M. M., pages 60–61.)

As men begin to grow civilized, they cease to be satisfied with mere tabus, and substitute divine commands
and prohibitions. The Decalogue begins: 'God spoke
these words and said.' Throughout the Books of the
Law it is the Lord who speaks. To do what God forbids is wicked, and will also be punished. Thus the
essence of morality becomes obedience. The fundamental obedience is to the will of God, but there are
many derivation forms which owe their sanction to the
fact that social inequalities have been divinely insti-
tuted. Subjects must obey the king, the slaves their
master, wives their husbands, and children their par-

ents. The king owes obedience only to God, but if he fails in this or his people will be punished. When David took a census, the Lord, who disliked statistics, sent a plague, of which many thousands of the children of Israel died (I Chron. xxi). This shows how important it was for everybody that the king should be virtuous. The power of priests depended partly upon the fact that they could to some extent keep the king from sin, at any rate from the grosser sins such as worship of false gods. (H. S. E. P., page 33.)

Kant was never tired of pouring scorn on the view that the good consists of pleasure, or of anything else except virtue. And virtue consists in acting as the moral law enjoins, *because* that is what the moral law enjoins. A right action done from any other motive cannot count as virtuous. If you are kind to your brother because you are fond of him, you have no merit; but if you can hardly stand him and are nevertheless kind to him because the moral law says you should be, then you are the sort of person that Kant thinks you ought to be. But in spite of the total worthlessness of pleasure Kant thinks it unjust that the good should suffer, and on this ground alone holds that there is a future life in which they enjoy eternal bliss. If he really believed what he thinks he believes, he would not regard heaven as a place where the good are happy, but as a place where they have never-ending opportunities of doing kindnesses to people whom they dislike. (H. S. E. P., page 49.)

Kant invented a new moral argument for the existence of God, and that in varying forms was extremely popular during the nineteenth century. . . . The point I am concerned with is that, if you are quite sure there is a difference between right and wrong, you are then in this situation: Is that difference due to God's fiat or is it not? If it is due to God's fiat, then for God Himself there is no difference between right and wrong, and it is no longer a significant statement to say that God is good. If you are going to say, as theologians do, that God is good, you must then say that right and wrong have some meaning which is independent of God's fiat, because God's fiats are good and not bad independently of the mere fact that He made them. If you are going to say that, you will then have to say that it is not only through God that right and wrong come into being, but that they are in their essence logically anterior to God. You could, of course, if you liked, say that there was a superior deity who gave orders to the God who made this world, or you could take up the line that some of the gnostics took up—a line which I often thought was a very plausible one— that as a matter of fact this world that we know was made by the devil at a moment when God was not looking. There is a good deal to be said for that, and I am not concerned to refute it. (w. n. c., page 12.)

To a modern mind, it is difficult to feel enthusiastic about a virtuous life if nothing is going to be achieved by it. We admire a medical man who risks his life in an epidemic of plague, because we think illness is an evil, and we hope to diminish its frequency. But if illness is no evil, the medical man might as well stay comfortably at home. To the Stoic, his virtue is an end in itself, not something that does good. And when we take a longer view, what is the ultimate outcome? A destruction of the present world by fire, and then a repetition of the whole process. Could anything be more devastatingly futile? There may be progress here and there, for a time, but in the long run there is only recurrence. When we see something unbearably painful, we hope that in time such things will cease to happen; but the Stoic assures us that what is happening now will happen over and over again. Providence, which sees the whole, must, one would think, ultimately grow weary through despair. (H. W. P., page 255.)

When I was a child the atmosphere in the house was one of puritan piety and austerity. There were family prayers at eight o'clock every morning. Although there were eight servants, food was always of Spartan simplicity, and even what there was, if it was at all nice, was considered too good for children. For instance, if there was apple tart and rice pudding, I was only allowed the rice pudding. Cold baths all the year round were insisted upon, and I had to practise the piano from seven-thirty to eight every morning although the fires were not yet lit. My grandmother never allowed herself to sit in an armchair until the evening. Alcohol and tobacco were viewed with disfavour although stern convention compelled them to serve a little wine to guests. Only virtue was prized, virtue at the expense of intellect, health, happiness, and every mundane good. (P. F. M., page 3.)

For over two thousand years it has been the custom among earnest moralists to decry happiness as something degraded and unworthy. The Stoics, for centuries, attacked Epicurus, who preached happiness; they said that his was a pig's philosophy, and showed their superior virtue by inventing scandalous lies about him. One of them, Cleanthes, wanted Aristarchus persecuted for advocating the Copernican system of astronomy; another, Marcus Aurelius, persecuted the Christians; one of the most famous of them, Seneca, abetted Nero's abominations, amassed a vast fortune, and lent money to Boadicea at such an exorbitant rate of interest that she was driven into rebellion. So much for antiquity. Skipping the next 2,000 years, we come

to the German professors who invented the disastrous
theories that led Germany to its downfall and the rest
of the world to its present perilous state; all these
learned men despised happiness, as did their British
imitator, Carlyle, who is never weary of telling us that
we ought to eschew happiness in favour of blessedness.
He found blessedness in rather odd places: Cromwell's
Irish massacres, Frederick the Great's bloodthirsty per-
fidy, and Governor Eyre's Jamaican brutality. In fact,
contempt for happiness is usually contempt for other
people's happiness, and is an elegant disguise for hatred
of the human race. (P. F. M., page 215.)

Acknowledgements

The editor is especially grateful to Lord Russell for his kindness in reading and correcting major sections from the first draft of this book, and to Lord and Lady Russell for approving the final draft. The editor also wishes to thank the following persons for their generous help in preparing this anthology: Professor Alvan J. Obelsky of the University of Miami (Florida), Lydia Peterson, Karin Sandstrom, Gladys Lober, Marvin O. Hunt, Milton S. Wilson and his wife, Margaret Egner.

For arrangements made with various publishers whereby certain copyrighted material was permitted to be reprinted, and for the courtesy extended by them, the following acknowledgements are gratefully made:

George Allen & Unwin Ltd. and Simon and Schuster: for permission to use excerpts from Lord Russell's:

A History of Western Philosophy	(1945)
New Hopes for a Changing World	(1951)
Unpopular Essays	(1950)
Impact of Science on Society	(1953)
Nightmares of Eminent Persons	(1955)
Authority and the Individual	(1949)
Satan in the Suburbs	(1953)
Human Society in Ethics and Politics	(1954)
Portraits from Memory	(1956)
Why I Am Not a Christian	(1957)

George Allen & Unwin Ltd. and W. W. Norton and Company, Inc.: for permission to quote material from Lord Russell's:

Power: A New Social Analysis	(1938)
Education and the Social Order	
(English title)	(1932)

Education and the Modern World
(American title)
An Outline of Philosophy (English title) (1927)
Philosophy (American title)

Beacon Press: for permission to reprint excerpts from:

'The Political and Cultural Influence,' in *The Impact of America on European Culture*
(1951)

George Allen & Unwin Ltd. and Liveright Publishing Corporation: for permission to use excerpts from Lord Russell's:

Marriage and Morals   (1929)
The Conquest of Happiness   (1930)

The Oxford University Press, London and New York: for permission to use excerpts from Lord Russell's:

Religion and Science   (1935)

LOOK MAGAZINE: for permission to use excerpts from Lord Russell's article:

'What Is an Agnostic' in the November 3, 1953, issue.

COMMON SENSE: for permission to reprint excerpts from Lord Russell's:

'Why Radicals Are Unpopular'   (March 1936)

NEW YORK TIMES MAGAZINE: for permission to quote material from two articles by Lord Russell:

'To Face Danger Without Hysteria'
(January 21, 1951)
'The Science to Save us from Science'
(March 19, 1950)

UNITED NATIONS WORLD: for permission to reprint excerpts from Lord Russell's article:

'Boredom or Doom in a Scientific World'
(September 1948)

MENTOR Books of Special Interest

**OUT OF MY LIFE AND THOUGHT by Albert Schweitzer
With Postscript 1932-1949 by Everett Skillings**

The remarkable autobiography of one of the 20th century's greatest men; a musician, philosopher, theologian, and medical missionary in Africa. (#MP483—60¢)

**ETHICS IN A BUSINESS SOCIETY by Marquis W. Childs
and Douglass Cater**

A brilliant interpretation of a monumental inquiry into the nature of moral values in the modern world.
(#MT724—75¢)

**RELIGION AND THE RISE OF CAPITALISM
by R. H. Tawney**

The influences of religious thought on the social and economic structures of the world. (#MT507—75¢)

**DIALOGUES OF ALFRED NORTH WHITEHEAD
as recorded by Lucien Price**

Professor Whitehead converses about books, people, events, and ideas in this illuminating book by a long-time friend. (#MT586—75¢)

SCIENCE AND GOVERNMENT   by C. P. Snow

Through the story of the famous Tizard-Lindemann debacle of World War II, an urgent plea for a re-evaluation of the role of the scientist in government.
(#MP444—60¢)

THE UNDISCOVERED SELF   by C. G. Jung

The world-renowned psychiatrist discusses the predicament of man in this restless world and offers a solution through understanding of the inner self.
(#MT715—75¢)

THE MENTOR PHILOSOPHERS